MARCEL DUCHAMP

GLORIA MOURE

MARCEL DUCHAMP

EDICIONES POLÍGRAFA, S. A.

© *1988 Ediciones Polígrafa, S. A.*
Balmes, 54 - 08007 Barcelona (Spain)

Reproduction rights:
A.D.A.G.P., Paris - L.A.R.A., S. A., Madrid
Translation by Joanna Martinez

I.S.B.N. 84-343-0542-9
Dep. Legal: B. 32.844 - 1988 (Printed in Spain)

Printed in Spain by La Polígrafa, S. A.
Parets del Vallès (Barcelona)

CONTENTS

Introduction: Reflections on the correct critical viewpoint

Although the critical appreciations of Marcel Duchamp and his work that have appeared since the second decade of this century have not been very numerous, their assessments have certainly been varied. Both his personal life and his work have been the subject of controversy, with critical attitudes ranging from sterile veneration to sheer malice; in fact, only indifference has been absent from opinions concerning that world of diverse influences that make up the pervading Duchamp ethos. Everything about him was unique; and his own attitudes, his lifestyle, his thoughts and his specific creations form a private universe that is extremely simple, sincere and modest. But perhaps it is this singular quality, combining a rebellious attitude with the utmost respect for tradition, that makes any partial analysis of Duchamp inadequate, if not misleading, and produces — at least initially — a fairly impenetrable barrier to understanding, a barrier that at all events is more apparent than real. The key to eliminating this obstacle is to identify with the artist in his concerns, desires and convictions, and to spurn intellectualist interpretations, which are as arid as they are unproductive. In this way it becomes possible to form a coherent view of Marcel Duchamp's contribution to art.

Duchamp grew up in a cultured family environment in which, through his mother's influence, the plastic arts played an important part. This somewhat rarified atmosphere did not, however, mean that popular culture and humour were ignored or rejected, but rather brought with it a respect for authentic tradition that was deeply rooted and afforded Marcel in particular — and the Duchamps as a family — a certain distance and circumspection that enabled him to survive unscathed the cultural oppression of the late nineteenth and early twentieth centuries, and to comprehend early on the true signs of his time. Nevertheless, the real extent of that independent nature was not revealed until social and artistic conventions threatened the artist's own creative capacity. And it should be borne in mind, too, that during his youth a continual dissatisfaction with the prevailing approach to artistic creation — and, by extension, to the whole of life itself — certainly induced him to go his own way, despite having initially become closely involved with the avant-garde movements of the day, in both painting and sculpture. Such notorious events as Duchamp's works failing to find a place at the Salon des Indépendants in Paris played a considerable part, but they were by no means the principal cause of change, for his dissatisfaction went much deeper than mere resentment. The conventions that bore down on the sensibilities of Marcel Duchamp went beyond the superficial level of established social customs and cultural norms; they concerned the classification and interpretation of objects and phenomena, and, consequently, the role played by art and by the artist in all this. Failure to grasp the range of conventions that were actually relevant to the young Marcel Duchamp has, I think, led to unhelpful partial interpretations, which have in turn given rise to vain undertakings by many enthusiastic followers who have focused their attention on matters that either did not present problems or were simply never considered seriously as such by Duchamp himself. Indeed, he tended to ignore controversies rather than take part in arguments on topics that in fact had nothing to do with him.

As he very clearly stated in his 1957 lecture in Houston, Texas, he reserved for the artist an essentially intuitive role; it should not be forgotten, however, that intuition conflicts not with thought, but rather with comprehension, for it is an alternative to reasoning and the law of cause and effect. When Duchamp argued for the return of art to the world of ideas, he was advocating not intellectualization but a personal inner culture consistent with moral discipline, with an ethic that would not tolerate a self-satisfying and empty art — in as much as it was purely sensory — to which he felt opposed. He never spoke of converting but of returning, of going back to the great tradition. He hated the idea of Art as an autonomous concept. It was an attitude that was radically opposed to a certain type of art and its eager devotees, whilst at the same time being a righteous and ascetic affirmation that accepted the separation, the final divorce. For Duchamp the year 1912 marked the point of no return, after which coherent developments of his adopted position would in due course occur. In the course of that year, his *Nude Descending a Staircase* (fig. 42) was withdrawn from the Salon des Indépendants; Duchamp saw a performance of the play *Impressions d'Afrique* by Raymond Roussel, which — thanks to its use of word-play and stage spectacle — proved to be an illuminating experience; he spent much time in lucid reflection during his trip to the Jura mountains with Francis Picabia, and during his stay in Munich was to discover new ideas for his journey into the unknown; and, finally, in the United States his works were selected for the Armory Show in New York, and he was accepted without hypocrisy in a country that was open to everything yet demanded neither a 'rate of production' nor an obligatory presence in artistic circles, while at the same time shielding him from European cultural influences. One of the most obvious developments was his revolt against the archetypes of art and artists. But like everything about Duchamp, this attitude had two aspects; on the one hand, his disdain for servile compliance by artists with leading cultural conventions, a tendency which manifested itself and was evident in stylistic imitations and in the obsession with the breaking down of preconceived notions; and on the other hand, his defence of individualization, of singularity, of the independence of the artist and his works, for he believed that these possess a particular temporal dimension, related to inner vision and experience and involving a distancing from or delaying ('retardation') of the accumulative approach typical of the sophisticated concept of modernity. In this context, plastic 'non-action' loses its passive connotation and is subsumed in a creative continuity which, in the final analysis, must be likened to life itself or — as Duchamp symbolically put it — to breathing. He had perceived that modern conceit had fragmented both human thought and human action, and he was not prepared to accept the exaltation of the god-like super-artist who laid down the aesthetic patterns to be followed at any given moment. The act of creating was what was truly important, not the creator; hence this act could never have any corporate sanction. The possibility of creative activity had to be available to every individual, and an individual was what Duchamp himself simply tried to be. The fact that a particular artistic creation was well received or considered important was as of as little consequence to him as its being completely ignored. Hence Duchamp's ascetic temperament and lifestyle, his passion for even the humblest manual task.

In the years following World War II, critics tended to stereotype Duchamp in trite reviews that were too often accepted at face value by the art world, with the result that the overall assessment of him provided by André Breton, describing him as the 'demarcation line' between the contradictory forces of the 'modern spirit', and Willem de Kooning's astute definition of him as a 'one-man movement ... open for everybody' went unheeded. Thus, what predominated was a partial view that emphasized only the rebellious gesture of Duchamp clothed in passive disdain, and held him up as the effective destroyer of the whole tradition of art. However, his real influemce was very different, and our image of him has come to acquire a profile more in line with his militancy, which was itself as arrogant as the avant-garde bluster it sought to combat, and with his exploration and opening up of the possibilities of plastic configuration. It is therefore fairer and more sensible to study and analyze Duchamp and his work viewed from a wider and more positive standpoint, since this enables the concerns and convictions that constitute the central thread of his whole œuvre to be appreciated.

As we have said, having adopted a highly personal, individualist stance, which manifested itself in an anti-emotive approach to the plastic arts, restricted in expression and far from any 'physicalism', Duchamp proceeded to expand all the areas of creation within his reach. Thus, while in one sense he considered the receptive phase of a work as consubstantial with it, in another he magnified the procedural aspect of it; moreover, he integrated in one total concept of creativity the decisions, choices and actions of the creator, while at the same time giving the creator the opportunity of moving with maximum freedom in a universe of existing images and objects, using these and adapting them at his discretion as 'Readymades', employing unpredictable and varied techniques and materials, and placing equal value on the permanent and the transient, the powerful and the subtle, the grand and the mean. Duchamp demostrated with brilliant clarity that whilst every work has an element of meaning, it also possesses strictly plastic attributes that have no conceptual overtones at all. He underlined too, in passing, the fallacy of trying to isolate one thing from the other, for language, image and material inevitably go hand in hand, and therefore the best way to achieve greater plasticity is to shift in stages through the network of connections that such natural contact allows. The desire to create acts precisely on these 'hinges' between words and things that unite in an unbroken circle forms, colours, sounds and meanings. This method certainly disobeys normal rules in that it mocks the truth, but at all events it has a positive side for it lyricizes rather than destroys all efforts to classify experiences. It thus prevents any futile attempts to extract the nature of a work of art — something that is by definition obscure — by reductionism. This was why Duchamp always remained a figurative artist — in fact, he never even cared whether he was one or not, for this argument was not of the least concern to him. Nevertheless, his works present a contrast between their manifest plastic qualities and their immense ambiguity of meaning, and are therefore excellent abstractions. Thus, his cryptic note on the 'figuration of a possible' gradually begins to make sense when we explore his work in depth.

The fact that Marcel Duchamp worked on the pivot of modern contradictions, on the rotating hinges that continually cause the appearance of things to change in the eyes of the viewer, meant that his works possess the quality of an 'interstice', a subtle interval. This was a great help in solving with immense simplicity such secular conflicts in the plastic arts as those generated by ideas of time, movement, obverse and reverse, multiplicity of meanings and the expression of perceptible though unconfigurable dimensions, without having to invade terrains other than the purely artistic. The physical projection of this interstitial quality was basically developed through the concepts of coincidence, instantaneousness and transition, which were to turn a considerable number of his works into 'instantaneously suspended encounters' that absorbed all these ideas without highlighting any one of them.

This extension of an artist's normal tasks, and the simultaneous preoccupation with fundamentally traditional matters in art, continued unaltered throughout Duchamp's life and can be clearly seen right through from his Cubist period up to his carefully planned Installation (figs. 129, 130) transferred after his death to the Philadelphia Museum of Art. It is so evident that the researcher is almost convinced that that amalgam of restless explorations constitutes in fact the theme itself rather than the particular motifs. This has two immediate consequences: on the one hand, the fact that individual works by Duchamp can very well be appraised and analyzed in isolation, but also have their place in a well-structured overall strategy that repeatedly links them together; and, on the other hand, the impracticality of applying to that structure any criteria of chronological progression, since the changes that occur between the works, differentiating them whilst at the same time connecting them, are due more to the idea of mutation in a continually reversible world than to any idea of a series of innovations.

The formative period

The first phase of Marcel Duchamp's artistic output was, not surprisingly, eclectic. Nevertheless, from his early sketches until 1910, and in occasional works produced the following year, one cannot speak of synthesis but rather of a period of experimentation and development of skills, which meant an attempt to exhaust in turn the possibilities of the style temporarily adopted. A review of this period based on a biographical analysis is at all events inevitable, for these years saw the emergence of certain elements that were to retain their influence throughout the artist's creative career and were to lead to results that were of fundamental importance. It is characteristic of Duchamp that, having moved to Montmartre in 1904 (his brothers Gaston and Raymond were both already in Paris), he should remain in rather unproductive contact with conventional art circles. His wayward behaviour while studying painting at the Académie Julian and his failure to pass the entrance examination to the École des Beaux-Arts were in themselves more than mere incidents, as was his enthusiastic dedication to producing satirical cartoons for various periodicals. His sense of irony was to become a permanent form of exorcism to enable him to escape from any stylistic stereotyping. Hence the ease with which he passed through Cubism, his tenacious and solitary progress towards the *Large Glass* (fig. 79), or the sudden appearance of the Readymades. Examples of this controlled irony are his treatment of *Portrait (Dulcinea)* (fig. 29), the choice of graphic elements in the *Large Glass*, the effort required in viewing *Étant donnés...* (figs. 129, 130), and the subtle alteration of existing objects. Despite his masterly control of colour, as seen in his Fauvist or Post-Impressionist works, Duchamp was to maintain his early fondness for drawing. In this respect we should note the essence of draughtsmanship in the progression from *Nude Descending a Staircase* (fig. 42) to the *Bride* (fig 53), which accelerated rapidly during his two-month stay in Munich in 1912, or the preference for the type of dry technical drawing that is a feature of the elaborate work of the *Large Glass*. It is more than likely too that the 'snapshot' effect inherent in the work of illustrating periodicals had something to do with the concept of instantaneousness as a solution to conveying three-dimensional forms.

Overall, Duchamp's progress through various areas of interest during this formative period, instead of attempting a mixture of them all, sheds some light on a system that was to become habitual and which consisted in projecting the desired configuration by means of generic groups. The immediate usefulness of this method is that it enables the expressive force to be isolated from the tempting literary essence of the content — a path which various specialists have followed without much success, such is the 'plastic isolation' that Duchamp achieves in his works. The Boxes (figs. 111, 112) are an evident generic group, in the same way as the series of doors. Duchamp himself pointed out that eroticism should be considered as respectable an 'ism' as any other. What is more, there are motifs from this early period which, as a class, became a recurrent structural feature that was to appear throughout his creative life. The lamp entitled *Bec Auer* (fig. 121), an illustration from his schooldays (1903-04), was to reappear decades later in *Étant donnés..., The Knife-grinder* (fig. 59), drawn in 1904-05, is a schematic representation of the mechanics of revolution, later to be repeated in *Chocolate Grinder, No. 2* (fig. 70) and

Bicycle Wheel (fig. 65). The importance in this respect of the 1907 and 1908 drawings of nudes on a ladder (figs. 40, 41) is quite clear.

Having completely mastered Post-Impressionist techniques, Duchamp was struck by the aggressiveness of Fauvism and in particular by the work of Matisse. This doubtless signified an urge to move away from an exclusively visual approach and return to an appreciation of shape and form; but alongside the attraction to Fauvism and still within this period of stylistic see-sawing which he himself acknowledged, there was another notable and even more important influence. His aversion to the purely sensory included not only Impressionist techniques but also naturalism, for he felt very strongly the need to go beyond conventional reality. In this respect, Odilon Redon's motifs and his particular way of suspending subjects on the pictorial plane influenced Duchamp profoundly, to the point where he later admitted that it was in fact this that triggered off everything else. It would not be incorrect to state that, when it comes to explaining his progress towards the *Large Glass*, this relationship with Redon was to be as important as some of the discoveries made during the execution of *Nude Descending a Staircase*. In the 1910 portrait of his friend Dumouchel (fig. 16), the ironic articulation of the figure and the background, as well as the presence of a halo around the hand, are evidence of his probing the idea of meta-reality. Similar questions arise with regard to *Standing Nude* (fig. 19) and *Nude on Nude* (fig. 22) of 1910 and 1911. *The Bush* (fig. 20), of 1910-11, would seem to be an extremely important work, not only because of the symbolist execution of the figures in an aureole of burning bushes, but because the subject (an adolescent girl in virginal transit) relates to the spirit of the *Large Glass* and even more so to *Étant donnés*. . . .

The experiment with Cubism

Marcel Duchamp, Jacques Villon and Raymond Duchamp-Villon at Puteaux, 1913.

An assiduous frequenter of the gatherings held by his brothers in the Paris suburb of Puteaux, which were attended by leading theoreticians of the Cubist movement, Marcel Duchamp shared the group's concern with finding a new style of visual representation, with the introduction of movement into the plastic arts and, in general, with the whole subject of the inherent limitations of the flat picture plane. Without any doubt whatever, this period — which could loosely be called Cubist, and which only lasted for that single year of 1911 — no longer answered to the description 'eclectic', which we have used in connection with his earlier work. Duchamp considered very seriously the Cubist approach, and his brief involvement with the movement should never be considered as a mere experiment in style. Like all artists in his circle at that time, he shared the same restlessness; but conscious as he was of the upheaval they were causing, he was nonetheless aware of being part of something that was hesitant and unsure of itself, limited by the relativity of events and discoveries. As he himself said, the theoretical and practical process of the 'decomposition' of forms that had already been suggested by Cézanne and developed by the Fauves was, with the Cubists, a gradual process surrounded by obscurity. Duchamp, however, maintained from the outset his deeply rooted independence, and, far from acting as an effective acolyte, he was to experiment with his own version of the subject. In this sense, the symbolist connection noted earlier and even the inveterate irony of a cartoonist were to place him at a sufficient distance not to feel himself irrevocably seduced by a ferment of creative activity which, both at a personal level as well as from the point of view of the works produced, constituted one of the most authentic, sincere and honest movements of contemporary art.

In the unfinished oil of 1911, *Apropos of Little Sister* (fig. 26), one can see a clear breakdown of forms that has no connection with any time sequence,

Suzanne, Mme Duchamp, Marcel and Yvonne, 1896.

whereas in *Yvonne and Magdeleine in Tatters* (fig. 27) the orthodox Cubist imprint is much harder to identify. In the latter work the profiles of the artist's sisters are drawn, as if torn up, on various scales, without relating them to any compositional plan at all. They appear to be 'floating' on the background, and seem to be outlined at the points where they intersect it. Although the work was executed at the peak of Duchamp's Cubist period, it contains elements that had been tried out earlier and, more importantly, it involved the search for immaterialness and the introduction of an ironic humour based on style as an instrument of form rather than of content. In *Sonata* (fig. 28), also executed in 1911, he already shows the beginnings of his own individual interpretation of Cubism: paticularly notable is the centred structure, which, although it appears to be cruciform, is in fact the typical fan shape that he was to use later. Moreover, despite the angular planes, the colours are soft and misty, which creates the sensation that the images could be floating. It is in *Dulcinea* (fig. 29) that the dynamic explosion of parts is achieved by a subtle and respectful irony of style. The fan of revolving figures shows the anonymous woman in five shifting positions as her clothing is gradually removed. A prime example of 'detheorization' and at the same time a personal statement, *Dulcinea* is a direct forerunner of what was to culminate in *Nude Descending a Staircase* (fig. 42). Equally premonitory and equally important as the keystone of stylistic consolidation are the illustrations that Duchamp did at that time based on various poems by Jules Laforgue, not so much because they also anticipate the theme of a person on a staircase or because they show for the first time successive states of mechanical progression, but because Laforgue — that master of wit, indifference and free verse — may, with Roussel, have had a decisive influence on Duchamp when it came to conceiving the method of 'pictorial nominalism' by means of which he managed to depict his universe of images in transit.

After *Dulcinea*, Duchamp returned to the theme of the chess players that he had previously recreated at Puteaux. The static subject matter of *Portrait of Chess Players* (fig. 35) links him more closely to orthodox Cubism, as occurred with *Sonata*, but the many sketches for this work seem to take him beyond what he achieved in *Dulcinea* and to point to certain aspects that were to be very relevant once he had abandoned conventional painting. In pallid tones against an undefined background (he painted the picture by gaslight) the images of the players are broken down into overlapping transparent planes, whilst a brief reference to the chess pieces appears suspended in the centre. However, *The Chess Players* (fig. 32), a related oil which is smaller than the final version, shows quite clearly how Duchamp was already as much concerned with differentiating the facets of an image in a two-dimensional space as with achieving an undifferentiated space in which the figures and colours were to 'appear' rather than be 'decomposed'. In this oil study the figures, although centred, do not predominate any more than do the groups of pieces, and the overall result is to produce a sense of movement that is mental rather than physical. In his progression from *Nude Descending a Staircase* to the *Large Glass*, Duchamp considered carefully the application of different 'speeds' to suit the various images within a single composition. And this method of contrast was already discernible in the carefully composed *Portrait of Chess Players*.

Despite his nonconformity, Marcel Duchamp was in sympathy with the theorizings of the Puteaux group, and he therefore considered the system of 'elementary parallelism' that he developed at the same time as *The Chess Players*, and which culminated in 1911 with a self-portrait, *Sad Young Man in a Train* (fig. 39), to be a commendable achievement. Although this work made less of an impact than *Nude Descending a Staircase*, it marked the beginning of a series of paintings governed by the idea of movement as understood physically, which was to end in 1912 with *The King and Queen Surrounded by Swift Nudes* (fig. 49). The self-portrait generated 'slabs' intersecting in space, those caused by the movement of the person mingling with those produced by the movement of the train. The technique used in *Nude Descending a Staircase* is exactly the same, and it was most probably not so much the method that caused the difficulties with the Salon des Indépendants as the title, which — although quite innocuous today — was a provocative one in those days. Despite this experience, Duchamp went on to explore the promising possibilities suggested by the two works. They signified, on the one hand, the introduction of the dissociation between title and image as an additional element and, on the other, a reduction of the creative approach, taking it back to its symbolist ideal and leading it unerringly towards a world of interior visions that are minimally and cryptically expressed, without the need for narratives or visually obvious configurations. The chronophotographs of Muybridge and Marey were then in fashion, and 1912 was also the year in which the Futurists first exhibited in Paris, but despite an apparent formal similarity to the latter that was more a matter of emphasis, Duchamp was not interested in producing cinematic effects, for he rejected any method of sensory 'impression'. He had, quite simply, proceeded to decompose forms, not in any attempt to obtain an effect of simultaneity but in order to present an absolutely static expression of movement in terms of its relationship with a succession of two-dimensional spatial planes. In fact, this 'elementary parallelism' freed him, as he proceeded to refine it, from the restrictions of a static medium of expression, for it gave him the idea, both technically and poetically, of the instantaneous effect produced by the intersection of planes. In this new ambit — a nude depicted in 'slabs', as it were — any symbolism, however banal and minimal, acquired maximum expressive proportions. Duchamp's manuscript entitled 'Enfant Phare' ('Headlight child'), written as a result of his journey by car to the Jura mountains in 1912, was to demonstrate the extent to which the creative spark of the new space of planar intersection had richness and strength, and to what point it also signified a happy blend of language and image in an undefined context.

At the end of 1911, for reasons that were purely domestic and devoid of any intellectual purpose, Duchamp produced a work that was to prove a decisive turning point. For his sister's kitchen he executed a small oil painting depicting a coffee-mill (fig. 37). The circular movement of the handle on top is shown in diagrammatic form and the apparatus is drawn in plan and elevation superimposed one upon the other. The combination of decomposition of forms and cold technical design, together with the simultaneous view of different planes, is a compendium of revelations. Here are the first signs of the rotating hinge, so loved by Duchamp for its technical and lyrical qualities, which is behind the physical and poetical solution of the *Large Glass*. In this sense, seeing a performance of Raymond Roussel's *Impressions d'Afrique* the following year (1912) gave Duchamp a feeling of support and liberation in pursuing his self-imposed role as a transformer of images and meanings through the mechanisms provided by his own surroundings and culture.

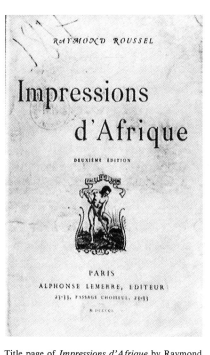

Title page of *Impressions d'Afrique* by Raymond Roussel. Bibliothèque Nationale, Paris.

Towards the configuration of desire

The incipient counterpoint suggested in 1911 in *The Chess Players* (fig. 32) by the 'circulation' or 'floating' of chess pieces around the players was developed by Duchamp — after painting *Nude Descending a Staircase* — in the series of works he completed before his visit to Munich in July and August 1912. In the small drawing *Two Personages and a Car* (fig. 45) one can see how the kinetic contrast is more pronounced and the immobility offset against the idea of acceleration, thus revealing a certain desire to achieve the plastic expression of an extreme situation. The idea hinted at in *Two Nudes: One Strong and One Swift* (fig. 44) is conveyed more definitively in the oil *The King and Queen Surrounded by Swift Nudes* (fig. 49). The irony of the titles demonstrates the use of a parallel linguistic acceleration, which was thereafter always to accompany the birth of images. The statically decomposed chess pieces are surrounded by a 'flow' of linear developments that have the appearance of a different tempo. This dynamic contrast was later to be replaced by an expression of metaphysical instantaneousness which would poetically sum up an intention of movement, but the 'swift nudes' are an early sign of a concept that was later used at will — the idea of the impossibility of any encounter (in this case between the king and queen) within the same space. This concept became a guiding principle that was to underlie the conception of the *Large Glass* and *Étant donnés...* and the birth of the Readymades, and would serve to illustrate the relationship between the individual and an unattainable reality.

While in Munich, Duchamp made a sudden move away from the kind of works he had produced immediately beforehand in Neuilly, where he lived from 1908 to 1913; those works show a certain exhaustion of the method of 'elementary parallelism' initiated in 1911, for it should be remembered that the 'accelerations' tended unerringly (in the end) towards a poetical universe rather than to making a physical and static statement. The use of intersecting planes in space was dropped, whilst the Cubist inheritance disappeared almost completely except for tones and colours. In the drawing *The Bride Stripped Bare by the Bachelors* (fig. 47) Duchamp still combined certain elements of kinetic demultiplication with the poetical-mechanical transformation of images, but the inscription 'Mécanique de la pudeur / Pudeur mécanique' ('Mechanism of chastity / Mechanical chastity') is an indication of the change that had taken place. However, in *Virgin, No. 1* and *Virgin, No. 2* (figs. 51, 52) the composition is already virtually static, although full of tensions produced by the mechanical-visceral execution. In *The Passage from Virgin to Bride* (fig. 50) and particularly in *Bride* (fig. 53) the absence of any realistic reference is total. In both works Duchamp appears to depict the interior of real images (which was to lead to the whole theory of the *Large Glass*). The *Bride* is imbued with symbolism, but the process of transformation of the motifs used is such as to achieve an extremely high degree of abstraction, eliminating specific symbolic references. The incandescent skeleton suggests a state of (erotic) desire and therefore illustrates an idea, a concept, of the solicitous bride. With this work Duchamp felt himself finally liberated, but instead of resting on his laurels he proceeded to 'escape forward'. There in Munich, the general plan of what the *Large Glass* was to be began to take shape. Duchamp knew what that meant: he had to go to ground, to experiment at length with untried techniques. As soon as he was back in Paris, he started work in the Bibliothèque Sainte-Geneviève, where he was able to do all the research he wanted, especially into perspective, for his ambitious projects.

Setting off alone

Up till now — that is to say, until the visit to Munich — we have been obliged to follow events in strict chronological order, starting with the various creations of Duchamp's formative years, described above as 'eclectic', and continuing with the succession of works produced during his brief Cubist phase, when he still retained his enthusiasm for and confidence in the historical avant-garde. After his return to Paris in 1912, however, everything changed, both in the realm of plastic creation and in his attitude to the socio-cultural environment. The three concepts of initiation, termination and repetition disappeared from Duchamp's *modus operandi* and were replaced by a sort of continuous, undifferentiated block, only faintly divided into stages by his inner experience. The commitment was therefore total, and much more far-reaching than mere intellectualization. The raised hand of the painter — gesturing, hedonistic and retinal — was replaced by the manual skills of the craftsman applied to dry, impersonal techniques, and by a plan of configuration that was the result of 'thinking with the eyes' in the manner of the classical artists. From the representation-recording of reality in accordance with meanings relevant to the predominant cultural discourse, Duchamp finally turned to delving into the lyrical transformation of reality; to do this, however, he did not recreate his dreams but placed himself within the web of words and things, releasing his inner impulse but containing his joys and sufferings in a disciplined manner. In that context, doing was as important as choosing or deciding. It was a matter of applying creative energy to the relatively frail edifice of conventional knowledge. Consequently, it meant attaching a value to chance, sometimes using it and as other times assisting it, so as to achieve unexpected results. It also meant considering the perception of something as part of a more unitary reality. All in all, it implied regarding the actions and reflections of the subject, as well as the substance of the objects surrounding it, as fluid and changing, stable only for a fleeting moment. Thus, a work becomes an apparition, not of reality but of a changing appearance of reality. The creator must always keep his distance and maintain his neutrality, setting aside his specific likes and tastes. In this way the work will be generated by desire, but the result is unlikely to be as specific as that desire. It was precisely this that led Marcel Duchamp to speak (in his 1957 talk in Houston, 'The Creative Act') of a certain 'art coefficient', which increases in proportion to the difference between what the artist 'intended to realize and did realize', and was of course incapable of rational explanation. From 1913 onwards this individualist and militant approach, which had already been glimpsed before, was adopted by Duchamp without hesitation. Having eliminated — or rather, ignored — conventionalisms, the creator and his creation blend into one without having to resort to nineteenth-century aestheticism, whilst art is diluted in life, making modern divisions and specializations seem mere trivialities. From this time on, all Duchamp's works were to revolve around this idea of totality and relativity.

Words and images

Given its active place on the rotating hinge of words and images (in the manner of Roussel), Duchamp's œuvre in general has linguistic, though not literary, connotations on the premise that language continually intrudes into the plastic arts, encroaching upon the visual. In a couple of highly significant texts (figs. 81, 82) — *The* (1915) and *Rendez-vous of Sunday, February 6, 1916...* (1916) — produced with great effort, he tried to eliminate all meaning so that the words would be without 'any echo of the physical world'. In the score *Musical Erratum* (fig. 63) of 1913 the plastic transfer is more obvious. In this work of fortuitous meaning and semantic ambiguity, Duchamp proceeded to select at random a French dictionary definition (in this case the verb *imprimer*, 'to print') and to set the words to music for three voices using notes picked, again at random, out of a hat. The main object of the work is not the music but rather the application of chance mechanics based on the number three (a metaphoric, pre-Socratic and prime number that he was to use continually as a rule of composition), in order to isolate the phonetic value and construct a kind of 'musical sculpture' on the basis of words. In one of the marginal notes included in the *Green Box* (fig. 111) of 1934, Duchamp clearly establishes his 'conditions of a language'. It is a matter of obtaining 'prime' words (by analogy with numbers, those that are 'divisible only by themselves or by unity'), for which he envisages the substitution of new schematic signs and proposes the use of different colours for the various syntactic elements. Elsewhere, in *In the Infinitive* (1967), he suggests film images of parts of very large objects in close-up to replace words with a 'dictionary' of 'signs' free of conventional linguistic associations. These signs, which are absolutely resistant to attack by meanings and all rules of syntax, would constitute what he called 'pictorial nominalism'. Earlier, in the short film *Anémic Cinéma* (1925-6), he had returned to the subject with the appearance on the screen of rotating discs bearing spirals of colours and words (figs. 106, 107).

However, despite taking the linguistic substratum and using it confidently in the manner of Laforgue, Brisset, François Villon, Jarry and Roussel, he never once crossed the boundaries of genres when searching for the most appropriate form of expression. If in the two texts referred to above (*The* and *Rendez-vous*) he restricted himself to the written word in the same way as occurred with the definitions of *'inframince'* and 'transformer' (to which we will return later), the Boxes are spaces of 'protoplastic' writing in themselves and must be evaluated as such. It is true that the *Green Box* was sarcastically described as a catalogue-guide to the *Large Glass*, something like a department store catalogue, but any reader who examines the notes — and the same is true of the *Box of 1914* (fig. 66) or of the *White Box (In the Infinitive)* mentioned above — can see roughly what the 'effort of configuration' is. In these Boxes, Duchamp transforms into a work what, before its artistic execution, had been a potential work, destroying with extreme ease the conventional idea of the 'beginning' and underlining the validity of the concept of the 'open-ended work'.

There are two parallel creations that exemplify the plastic-linguistic symbiosis whilst at the same time denouncing the potentially pernicious nature of such an inseparable union. One of these, a key work, is the creation of Duchamp's female *alter ego* under the arbitrary name of Rrose Sélavy, who was to recreate the androgynous nature of all creativity. As publisher of outrageous puns and owner of the copyright in various Readymades, she attempted to stave off the fragmentation that language and its patterns produce in the human being, converting the world into a bachelor unable to cohabit with reality. Her name appeared in its definitive version when Duchamp wrote the punning phrase 'Pi qu'habilla Rrose' on Picabia's *L'Œil cacodylate* (1920), since the French word 'arrose' required two R's. From this, two phrases were to emerge: 'aRrose Sélavy' (art is life) and 'Rrose Sélavy' (Eros is life). Eroticism, as a genre, was the only ambit of perception of dimensions that could be experienced but not configured. Strangely, the linguistic ferment that the androgynous sharpshooter had generated completed the circle of knowledge, condemning it to an eternal (though changing) return and expelling it from all linearity. The second work is *Three Standard Stoppages* (figs. 74, 75); authentic examples of 'canned chance' and indeterminate patterns, they are the true measures of the world of Duchamp described in this text, 'It is my most important work,' he himself said. The *Stoppages* succeed in measuring poetry and heightening the grandeur of the minimal. A brief description will suffice: three threads, each a metre in length, are dropped from a height of one metre on to a horizontal surface, their resulting deformed shapes are glued on pieces of canvas, which are in turn fixed to glass panels; each is accompanied by a wooden 'rule' with a curved outline conforming to the shape of each 'unit of length'. The whole is enclosed in a croquet box, 'to preserve them from other measurements'. Never perhaps have all the conventions been flouted in a more beautiful manner!

Rrose Sélavy, 1917. Photograph by Man Ray.

Readymades

There can be no doubt about the legitimate plastic-linguistic nature of the Readymade as a genre. As we have seen earlier when referring to the notes on 'prime' words, objects were to be used to generate signs corresponding to words; the Readymades are thus a paradigm of 'pictorial nominalism'. Indeed, suitably designed existing objects were to have been used to produce the bachelor messages in the *Large Glass* (though due to technical complications this was not done). It should be noted, in addition, that the decontextualization of objects (by means of dysfunction) runs parallel with semantic dissociation; that alliterations and unexpected titles are an essential feature of a good number of Readymades; and, finally, that Rrose Sélavy — nominalist *par excellence* — is often involved in selecting them. All these factors underline anew the cohesion of Duchamp's plastic corpus as a whole, but the Readymades have a couple of additional characteristics — one obvious, the other less so — which merit special mention on account of the repercussions they caused at the time. In the first place, these works plainly, literally and radically constituted a defiance of contemporay artistic convention and its pomposities. This iconoclastic function is so obvious as to need no further elaboration, for anyone can easily imagine what it must have meant in the 1920s or 1930s to present a household utensil as a work of art in a conventional gallery. It should, however, be pointed out that this element has been over-emphasized by the critics, to the extent that this aspect has been considered the only important one. The second characteristic, on the other hand, is a positive one, for it widened the scope of creativity. The key to the Readymade lies in the choice of the object itself. In the notes in the *Green Box*, Duchamp mentions the importance 'of timing, of this snapshot effect', each object being inscribed with relevant details of date and time as information (like an event). In this way the act of choosing takes on the characteristics of a 'delay'. In the *White Box* a note dated 1913 asks 'Can one make works which are not works of "art"?', and Duchamp goes on to speak of objects observed through a shop window, pointing out that the choice is a two-way one in the sense that the window also demands something from the viewer. Nevertheless, the demands made by the object upon the creator-selector are not based on attraction — which depends on the latter's taste — but on absolute indifference, on neutrality, in other words on a complete absence of good or bad taste (aesthetics), or total 'anaesthesia'. Even in his early notes, Duchamp was cautious about the number of Readymades he produced (per year) for he feared that if there were too many they might, in combination, end by creating a new aesthetic instead of being linked merely by indifference and the fact of having no artistic pretensions.

Bicycle Wheel (fig. 65), the original version of which dates from 1913, is an excellent example of selection by indifference (the artist having lived with the wheel in his Paris studio) and has the advantage that, although the work was extremely iconoclastic, its ambiguous symbolism went some way to softening its impact. Nevertheless, the elegant simplicity of the combination of wheel and stool, the vertical form and the overall creative connotations (which were probably to have important consequences) such as the rotary movement or the virtual structural effect of the spokes when the wheel is seen in motion, give it a markedly sculptural character, which Duchamp himself never intended, except as regards the movement. On the other hand, *Bottlerack* (fig. 76) of 1914 or the snow-shovel entitled *In Advance of the Broken Arm* (fig. 77) of 1915, as well as the typewriter cover *Traveller's Folding Item* of 1916 (fig. 84) or *Hat Rack* (fig. 88) of 1917 — all of them intended to be suspended (weightless) — have an aesthetic 'hardness' (or lack of aesthetics) that is very considerable. The same applies to the metal *Comb* (fig. 80) of 1916, inscribed with the date and time of its selection; and to the coat rack nailed to the floor (fig. 89), the title of which, *Trap* (1917), is a typically ironic allusion by Duchamp both to the fact that the object had become a 'trap', continually stumbled over by visitors to his studio, and to the power of a suitably placed pawn to 'trip' an opponent's pieces in chess. The relative lack of 'assistance' (or intervention) in these objects prevents the hardness of their origin being concealed by inevitable linguistic or symbolic associations, but on the other hand this simplicity links them directly to the concepts of the *Large Glass*. In addition, the fact that they were all pieces to be suspended was a very early foretaste of mobile sculptures (the genre principally associated with Alexander Calder), and in the specific case of the typewriter cover opened the way for sculpture that is flexible, soft and portable.

Pharmacy (1914) was the first 'rectified' Readymade, making use of an existing print (fig. 67). The work's origin was opportunist and intellectualized: whilst travelling to Rouen by train, Duchamp sat looking out on a gloomy landscape with two small lights in the distance. On arrival, he purchased a print of a landscape and painted two luminous dots on it, one red and the orher green, like glass jars in a pharmacy — hence the title, through linguistic association. The rectification of the advertisement for 'Sapolin enamel' paints (1916-17), which turned into an extremely cryptic homage to Guillaume Apollinaire, *Apolinère Enameled* (fig. 90), was equally bizarre. The reference to multiple realms of iconographic and linguistic meaning appeared in a more suggestive way in 1921 in the rectification of the perfume bottle (fig. 100), where Rrose Sélavy (with logotype) appears on the label ironically describing the contents as 'Eau de Voilette' ('Veil water') and 'Belle Haleine' ('Beautiful breath'). Here, Rrose Sélavy can be related to the moustached *Mona Lisa* of 1919, 'voilette' (veil) to the *Bride*, and 'haleine' (breath) to the poetic condition of '*inframince*' (translatable as 'infra-thin'). The rectification of the *Mona Lisa* retitled *L.H.O.O.Q.* (fig. 95) is, from a generic point of view, on a par with *Pharmacy*, but the archetypal content of the support categorically precludes the requisite of neutrality noted above; moreover, the pun (in French) on the initials that make up the title reinforces the sacrilegious nature of the work. The urinal (fig. 86) entitled *Fountain* (1917) is a Readymade of a similar type as regards its pointed message, but is unaltered except for the addition of a signature; however, its sculptural appearance, the functional reference and the dissociation implied in the signature 'R. Mutt' are excellent examples of anartistic alliances. Both works must be included in the context of Duchamp's sympathy with the Dada movement, which he strongly supported through his relationship with Picabia, Man Ray and Tristan Tzara. The reviews *Rongwrong, The Blind Man, New York Dada* and *391* provide good examples of his involvement. If, in the glass flask (fig. 93) entitled *50 cc of Paris Air* (1919), aesthetic neutrality gives way to poetic subtlety, in some highly assisted Readymades formed of an amalgam of objects the artistic upheaval is replaced by a desymbolization brought about by assemblies that go way beyond the mere dissociation of inscriptions in the style of *Apolinère Enameled* for example. Thus, in *With Hidden Noise* (1916), two brass plates are bolted together, and imprisoned between them is a ball of string containing an unseen and unidentified object that moves and makes a noise when the piece is shaken (fig. 83). In *Why not Sneeze Rrose Sélavy?* (1921), a white-painted bird-cage contains cubes of marble (imitating sugar), a thermometer and a cuttlefish bone, whilst the inscription on the bottom of the cage is reflected in a mirror set in the base. In both works the overlap of the poetic and the objective is strong and parallels the puns that assist them, but in addition they clearly reveal an ironic recreation of the search for a tactile quality and of the effort of perception, which were at the very heart of Duchamp's approach and continually surfaced to a greater or lesser degree throughout his creative career.

For Duchamp aims precisely at that inevitable and endless effort in the 'picture' entitled *Tu m'* ('*You ... me*') (fig. 87) of 1918. It represents an amalgam of pictorial techniques developed by him, featuring a series of rhombuses, random measurements, a parallelepiped produced by these

Marcel Duchamp, Francis Picabia and Beatrice Wood in Coney Island, New York, 1917.

Why not Sneeze Rrose Sélavy?, 3rd version (one of eight replicas signed and dated 1964) of the original of 1921. Private collection, Paris.

measurements, and tracings of shadows of Readymades projected on to the canvas. The bottle-brush (directed quite clearly at the eye of the viewer) emerges from the split that is 'held together' with safety pins. The composition, with its title to be completed at will, is a two-dimensional compendium of multi-dimensional and allegorical spaces, for it should be remembered that in the *Large Glass* the shadows projected from various positions were to occupy the upper part like visual impulses from the lower half which are disorientated on account of the lack of dimensional 'dexterity' in a space that is not identical. The brush highlights the dependence on the relative viewpoint, for it appears as two-dimensional when observed from in front and three-dimensional when seen from the side, thus poking fun at the viewer. This household object appears to erupt from the surface of the encyclopaedic picture, but its source is still subject to a perceptual relativity and the resulting transformation of its image.

The Bride Stripped Bare by her Bachelors, Even (The Large Glass)

This unfinished work (figs. 78, 79), which Duchamp admitted growing tired of, occupied him from 1915 to 1923, although certain related sketches and pieces had appeared as early as 1913 (fig. 57). It is therefore open-ended in two senses: on the one hand it was abandoned while incomplete; and on the other its beginnings were physically undefined, as shown by the notes concerning it in the *Green Box* (fig. 111), compiled as an aid to viewing. With the help of the uniformed shapes of the 'malic moulds' (fig. 61) and the similarly titled gouache from the Munich period (fig. 47), we can associate the title with those scenes in fairground booths where the bride is surrounded by figures of uniformed bachelors that have to be knocked down; However, to be faithful to the spirit of their author, it is better not to apply specific meanings, since we are here faced with a whole system of multi-purpose signs that would fit any well-articulated subject matter (as the numerous attempts show) and which at all events is in itself a representation of pictorial nominalism. The work contains two distinct spaces — the upper one, which allows itself to be seen in its multi-dimensional and unitary perfection, and the lower one, condemned to the bachelorhood of its own configurations and driven by eroticism (as the driving force) in a desire to arrive at the 'totality' it cannot attain despite its being available. The *Large Glass* thus seems to be a celebration of the pre-Socratic paradox of reality (if it exists, it is not comprehensible; and if it is, it is inexpressible). The sexes most probably parallel the ideas of unity and fragmentation (female and male), whilst the contrast of language and imagery in the two spaces illustrates the nub of the drama in all its grandeur, for in the desire to know aroused by the erotic perception of every dimension, even the smallest, lies the nature of human creativity.

As Duchamp acknowledged, the *Large Glass* involved distancing himself from everything that had gone before, firstly because of his use of the 'delay' in glass, as compared with all known techniques of painting, and secondly because the work was a reappraisal of technical perspective, for in this lay the contrast with the Cubist experiment. The poetical mechanization was partly influenced by Roussel, but at the same time it provided an excellent visual definition for the abstractions and a way of avoiding irrelevancies and clichés by virtually abolishing meanings or even the need for meanings.

Part of the *Bride* (fig. 53) executed in Munich in 1912 was to be used to compose the mechanisms of the bride which, activated by the erotic desire originating in the lower section, are the reason for the imagined stripping.

The process was to prove a difficult one, involving the creation of wire shapes containing coloured material which produced a photographic effect. At any rate, the gearing of the bride is relatively small in comparison with the cinematic 'blossoming' (the Milky Way) that emanates from her. This flesh-coloured blossoming (or halo) is the result of the collision of the two 'appearances' of nudity — that is to say, the one produced by the stripping by the bachelors, and the one imagined by the bride herself. The 'coincidence' of appearances would give rise to the emission of moving messages composed of 'alphabetic units'. Three nearly square openings ('draught pistons') framed by the halo channel the letters of the alphabet to the point where they meet the images sent from below by the bachelors (the shapes of the three 'pistons' were achieved by photographing the outline of a piece of net curtain suspended above a current of warm air; see fig. 72).

Chocolate Grinder, No. 2 (fig. 70) of 1914 was the second work that Duchamp transferred to the *Large Glass*, this time to the bachelor (lower) part, and in its entirety. Although the visceral exaggeration of the *Bride* of 1912 is to some extent related to the artist's Cubist period, the *Chocolate Grinder* was, in Duchamp's own words, a real liberation. Drawn in perfect perspective, the three rollers rest on a plain Louis XV-style chassis and the cords of the drums are threads sewn into the canvas. Thus the illusionism and the painterly execution suddenly disappear. Moreover, although the function of this artefact within the bachelor apparatus is relatively unimportant, for it merely supports the beams that move the sleigh (or glider), the allegorical component is very strong and in fact sums up the whole concept of the *Large Glass*. The machine operates 'spontaneously' without anything or anyone to activate it, for the simple reason that 'the bachelor grinds his chocolate himself' — a truly onanistic premise of existence that conditions the interpretative relationship of the subject with everything surrounding it, whether persons or things, for it produces its own configurations. This philosophical interpretation of the chocolate grinder is doubtless correct, but the choice of the apparatus — or rather, of its image — was much simpler than that, for it was the result of Duchamp's fascination at seeing such a machine through a shop window in Rouen. This fascination was not on account of the subsequent metaphorical attribute but arose from his interest in developing a new technique. The bride, in the supernatural upper space, is not subject to specific dimensions; she expands and emits her alphabetical-amorous instructions as her desire for acceptance 'coincides' with the presumably electrical stripping activated by the bachelors, but she is self-sufficient and possesses her own supply of 'love gasoline'. Conversely, the bachelor apparatus, drawn in meticulous perspective and constructed with 'imperfect' images based on circles, squares, rectangles, etc., depends on two given parameters — falling water and illuminating gas — which, like the milk chocolate in the grinder, come from an unknown source.

On the same plane as the chocolate grinder is the trolley on runners, behind which are the 'malic moulds' that form the 'Eros's matrix'. The moulds, which were derived from illustrated catalogues that picture the uniforms expanded but empty of occupants, are filled with illuminating gas; they 'hear the litanies sung by the chariot' and would 'hallucinate rather onanistically' as a result of their own complexity being reflected back to then. In the pencil drawing of 1913 entitled *Cemetery of Uniforms and Liveries, No. 1* (fig. 58) and in *Bachelor Apparatus (plan)* (fig. 54), also executed in 1913, the eventual position worked out for the 'uniforms' in the *Large Glass* can be seen. At first there were eight, but Duchamp added the 'Station-master' so as to have a number that was a multiple of three. The organization of the polygonal layout was extremely painstaking, for the figures had to be placed in such a way that they did not overlap each other when transferred in perspective onto the glass. The height at which the moulds are placed was calculated above and below a common horizontal plane so that the 'point of sex' of each figure occurs at one of the vertices of the polygon. The illuminating gas with which they are filled issues forth from the top of each mould and crosses the 1 metre unit of length (standard stoppage) in the form of 'capillary tubes', which solidify (freeze) the liquid gas which emerges in unequal 'spangles' that are 'lighter than air' and deposit them in the centre of the first 'sieve'. The plan and elevation clearly show the spatial complexity of the set of apparatuses in relation to each other. The overall space is divided midway by the trolley-sleigh, the chocolate grinder and the elliptical spiral (the last never executed) that issues from the last sieve. The malic moulds appear to be outside the glass and projected on to it, as are the sieves and the beginning of the spiral, which are seen behind the machinery in the foreground. The glass itself thus becomes an axial plane, cutting a vertical section through some of the images. This infinitesimal cut by a two-dimensional space passing through a three-dimensional space is linked to the earlier elementary parallelism of *Nude Descending a Staircase* and establishes the principle of 'apparition of an appearance' or 'surface apparition'. This idea of cutting applies equally to the 'coinciding' images in the foreground and to the projected images (moulds and sieves). The forms are therefore suspended in both space and time; and it is an instantaneous coincidence that involves the application of two extraordinary creative concepts — the aforementioned 'apparition' and *'inframince'* (infra-thin) — which enable us to understand not only the use of glass as an interstitial space but also the complicated execution of the three selected works on glass (figs. 61, 62, 79) that still exist today: *Nine Malic Moulds* (1914-15), *Glider Containing a Water Mill in Neighbouring Metals* (1913-15) and the *Large Glass* itself, the first two being studies for the third.

Duchamp defines 'appearance' as the 'usual sensory evidence enabling one to have an ordinary perception' of an object. 'Surface apparition' is the 'image in n-1 dimensions of the essential points of this object of n dimensions'. This apparition looks like a mould that facilitates the making of this object, a mould being, 'from the point of view of form and colour, the negative (photographic)', and 'from the point of view of mass, a plane (generating the object's form by means of elementary parallelism) composed of elements of light'. The 'apparition' would form the 'appearance' in the opposite sense to the use of elementary parallelism in *Nude Descending a Staircase*. The colours of the apparition are 'native' or intrinsic to the object and 'will determine the real colours which will change because of the exterior lighting'.

If Duchamp used glass instead of some other material, it was because it is the material best suited to the representation or momentary arresting of a 'continuum' of greater dimensionality captured in a two-dimensional axial plane. The layers of colour, applied from behind the glass, were built up as 'negatives' of the apparent colours and reflections were avoided by using lead foil. This anti-retinal quality is enhanced by the configuration of the images in reverse. It is particularly evident in the 'malic moulds': the uniforms and liveries of Eros's matrix cannot be precisely identified by their apparent aspect because this would be behind the mould as represented in the *Large Glass*.

At all events, the use of the phrase 'axial plane' is more graphic than conceptual; 'interval' would be more appropriate, since the *Large Glass* is a 'repose that develops' from an almost immaterial poetry defined by the differences between two reversible aspects of a single thing or phenomenon. The term that, according to Duchamp, would be considered linguistically as an adjective rather than a noun is the hermetic though suggestive *'inframince'*. He very clearly considered that a picture executed on glass seen from the unpainted side belonged in this category, but he generously provided descriptions of several other cases that help us to understand this point, a phenomenon which we have in fact all experienced at some time or other: the different aspects of the same object — the warmth of a chair after one has got up from it, the difference in size between two objects cast from the same mould, the faint rubbing sound made when walking in corduroy trousers, the difference between how a work sees the viewer and how the viewer sees the work, or the ability of tubes of paint to be turned into a picture. Thus, the *Large Glass* — like all *inframinces* — operates at the interstice; at the interstice of concentrated poetical and expressive intensity, but in the margin of scientific and linguistic knowledge. It is a minimal aesthetic, but minimal in the sense of the conventionally understood motif rather than of the different ways of recreating it or representing it. We all know the important role that little-noticed words and things may play in basic failures or in the making of extraordinary discoveries. Perhaps this was why Duchamp proposed a 'transformer intended to utilize little wasted energies' — such as the excess pressure on a switch, the exhalation of tobacco smoke, the falling of tears, the sound of nose-blowing or sighing — among other powerful and ironic subtleties that go unnoticed.

In the *Large Glass* the illuminating gas passes from each malic mould along a tubular 'unit of length', is solidifed and formed into 'elemental rods' which are broken down into spangles that are lighter than air — another example of *inframince* — and tend to rise. But they are deposited in the centre of the first sieve (parasol) and pass through a succession of parasols that are a 'reversed image of porosity'. The spangles, turned through a 'sort of labyrinth of the three directions', become disorientated and lose any 'awareness of position'; as a result, they can no longer retain their individuality and merge together to become a liquid.

While the 'improvement' of the illuminating gas is going on, the sleigh on runners of 'emancipated metal' (which is free of 'all gravity in the horizontal plane') recites the 'onanistic litanies' as it moves back and forth. On one side a system of springs (not included in the work) returns it to its initial position; on the other side, between the runners and resting on an axle connecting it to the chocolate grinder, a water wheel (with the water coming from somewhere above the moulds) operates a complicated mechanism based on a pulley system fitted with weights (varying in density according to whether they are rising or falling), which in turn permit the lowering of a hook made of a material of 'oscillating density'; this causes the sleigh to move towards the chocolate grinder and activates the opening of the scissors, so releasing a weight with nine holes in it, which on descending (falling) causes the liquefied gas emerging from the sieves to splash in a 'sculpture of drops', each drop being returned 'mirrorically' up towards the bride's domain (this system, along with the whole operating mechanism of the trolley, was never executed). The images of the regulated drops would be transformed with the aid of an optical prism, an element which — together with two other projected mechanisms (the 'boxing match' and the 'handler of gravity') — never materialized. Since the bachelor machine possesses only 'ordinary skill', the sculpture of drops that should have reached a single 'target' corresponding to the vanishing point of perspective, is demultiplied into nine separate 'shots' (three demultiplication points and three attempts from each) that do appear in the *Large Glass*. In this zone the commands of the bride were to join with the images of the bachelor area, but in practice no understanding between the upper and lower spaces will ever be achieved, for there will always be an *inframince* separating them.

In order to produce the labyrinth of sieves, Duchamp allowed the glass to gather dust for months and then fixed it with varnish — resulting incidentally in *Dust Breeding* (fig. 98), the excellent slow-exposure photograph by Man Ray taken in 1920 — and cleaned the remaining area. In the case of the *Oculist Witnesses*, the procedure was equally laborious, for he first had the chosen area of the glass silvered, then marked the optical charts on it using carbon paper and proceeded to remove the surplus metal deposit. The unperspectivized circle above them should have contained a magnifying lens, but this was not done.

Partly through tiring of the work and partly on principle, Duchamp left the *Large Glass* unfinished. As the work was in itself a section of a continuum, there was no reason to complete it with an articulated system, for like a 'clock in profile' it 'includes all the dimensions of duration'. Duchamp tried to 'avoid all formal lyricism' and to attain 'beauty of indifference' in painting via precision of execution; comprehension of a scenography was not among his aims. A paradigm of pictorial nominalism, the *Large Glass* is a 'tautology in acts'. If they were not told, viewers would never think it unfinished; if they did think so, something would be amiss.

Further extensions

There is a relative coincidence between Duchamp's abandoning of the *Large Glass* and the emphasis he placed on the game of chess, to the extent that critics have generally seen it as an aggressive gesture against art. However, in the context of a distancing from long-established conventions, this emphasis has a positive aspect — and a plastic aspect too — if we consider that Duchamp's outlook in the 1920s was a complete symbiosis of art and life. He said that when he played chess, competing was of no importance to him; on the other hand, playing a game was like 'designing something or constructing a mechanism', and the game itself was 'very plastic', for playing was a mechanical reality in the manner of drawing. Beauty was the 'imagining of movement or gesture' (as in the *Large Glass,* for example). The complicated treatise on chess that he wrote with Vitaly Halberstadt in 1932 (*L'Opposition et les cases conjuguées sont réconciliées*; fig. 110) is basically full of poetry, for like most of his plastic works it is a coincidental reconciliation in an extreme case, a real *'inframince'* of chess. Moreover, the cover of the book was designed by Duchamp as a negative of the shadows projected obliquely by the letters that make up the title.

In fact, the lithographic edition of *Obligations pour la roulette de Monte-Carlo* (fig. 103), produced jointly by Marcel Duchamp/Rrose Sélavy in 1924 and generally catalogued as a rectified Readymade, has strong links with *Cases conjuguées*. Although it was less fascinating than chess, Duchamp played around with random mechanics for a considerable time, in much the same way as he did with the units of length. In a letter to Doucet he insisted on the pictorial nature of his experiments with roulette. *Obligations*, in addition to containing a photograph by Man Ray of a Duchamp altered with shaving cream, had imprinted on it in the background the phrase 'Moustiques domestiques demistock', which appears in spiral form on a disc in *Anémic Cinéma*, thus underlining the endlessly pivoting hinge of multi-dimensionality.

Marcel Duchamp and Man Ray in a scene from René Clair's film *Entr'acte*, 1924.

While he was still busy working on the *Large Glass*, the pivotal picture *par excellence*, and shortly before producing *Tu m'*, in which the corkscrew (spiral analogy) appears projected anamorphically, Duchamp experimented with moving spirals. This form illustrates the concept of eternal return, the onanistic condemnation of life and of configuration, the dimensional leap from one plane to another — simple as regards language though difficult to achieve visually — but technically it also permits the appearance of 'virtual volume'; the kinetic effect acts in the same way as tricks of perspective do with regard to form. In the motor-driven *Rotary Glass Plates (Precision Optics)* of 1920 (figs. 96, 97), Duchamp decomposes the spiral in depth and activates the painted glass plates in order to produce the effect of a volume suspended in space. In the *Discs Bearing Spirals* of 1923 (fig. 104) and *Rotoreliefs (optical discs)* of 1935 (fig. 105) the idea of 'optical relief' is developed with the aim of reconstituting objects (a fish swimming around

Cœurs volants ('Fluttering Hearts'), 1936. Design for the cover of an issue of *Cahiers d'art* which included an important article on Duchamp's work by Gabrielle Buffet. Private collection, Barcelona.

Cover by Duchamp for *La Septième Face du dé/ poèmes-découpages* by Georges Hugnet, published in 1936.

André Breton and Oscar Domínguez standing in front of Duchamp's glass *Porte Gradiva*, 1937.

in a bowl, for instance; fig. 108). The kinetic effect of *Cœurs volants* (1936), or the experiment with the sensation of depth through coincidence produced by stereoscopics, are two further examples of the three-dimensional illusion that Duchamp was 'generically' trying out as part of his secular interest in the relativity of a specific viewpoint. Perhaps the most interesting work in this group is the film *Anémic Cinéma* (figs. 106, 107) of 1925 — mentioned earlier as an example of plastic-linguistic symbiosis — for it expounds very clearly not only the volumetric effect but the simultaneous-directional quality of the rotating (hinged) movement of visual or linguistic planes, a phenomenon related to the addition of another dimension, for it implies the reversal of images. The purpose of the anagram in the title is precisely to underline this fact.

Nevertheless, a change gradually took place in Duchamp which, although based on ideas similar to these earlier ones, involved a 'reversible' passage through the universe of image/matter by means of the broader concept of *inframince*, of the change to the three-dimensional effect, the abandoning of the use of glass as a support for continuous images, and the exacerbation of the inevitable visual effort — all coupled with an implied eroticism that was less descriptive and less removed. As an example of this we would point to a work considered to be of minor importance: the cover for *La Septième Face du dé / poèmes-découpages* by Georges Hugnet, published in 1936. Duchamp reproduced two cigarettes stripped of their paper wrapping, thus illustrating to perfection the idea of the negative mould in the *Large Glass*. The change referred to above signified moving to the other side of the mould, the side of the external appearance, though still preserving its quality of apparition and its corresponding attribute of *inframince*, for the three-dimensional appearance would continue to be an apparition by intersecting a greater dimensionality.

If the spiral was a motif and a subject that Duchamp recreated in careful detail, the same can be said for windows and doors. These constituted a double theme: in the first place, the visual effect, closely linked to the two-way association — the 'coition' — between the viewer and things viewed through a shop window, and secondly the translation (via the hinges) to another dimensional realm. In *Fresh Widow* (fig. 102) of 1920 Duchamp substitutes black leather (which had to be polished) for the glass panes in the window; and similarly in *La Bagarre d'Austerlitz* (fig. 101) of 1921 a solidly constructed window has white paint daubed on the glass. In both these works the linguistic dissociation of the titles reinforces the startling subject matter. In *Porte Gradiva* (1937), a pair of lovers (or rather their outline) serve to doubly delineate the doorway, in much the same way as the corresponding section of the *Large Glass*, so that — symbolically — on crossing it, the spaces are penetrated through the intersecting planes. The effect was even more obvious in the door that Duchamp had made for his apartment in the Rue Larrey in Paris. This two-way door led either from the bathroom to the studio or from the studio to the bedroom, for it was so constructed as to be simultaneously open and shut; the planar significance is quite clear, in that the door continuously connected two spaces. This latter experiment is related to Duchamp's designs for the 1938 Surrealist exhibition in Paris, which included revolving doors and a generally subdued lighting scheme. In another Surrealist exhibition he mounted, this time in New York in 1942, the visual impediment consisted of a web woven from 'a mile of string' that also made it difficult to move around. For his major last work, in fact, Duchamp chose a heavy wooden door, the only thing visible at first glance (fig. 129); it is only when the inquisitive viewer looks through the two holes situated at eye level in the door that his curiosity is satisfied by being able to view (through a camera obscura) the scene within (fig. 130). This is the culmination of the encounter, for he is captivated by the image of the nude woman and at the same time desires it.

Door, 11 Rue Larrey, Paris, 1927. Wooden door made by a carpenter under Duchamp's supervision. Private collection, Rome.

Design by Duchamp for the 'Exposition Internationale du Surréalisme', Galerie des Beaux-Arts, Paris, 1938.

Design by Duchamp for the exhibition 'First Papers of Surrealism', New York, 14 October-7 November 1942.

The path to
Étant donnés: 1, La chute d'eau; 2, Le gaz d'éclairage

Alongside the trend towards the obstruction of vision there was, as we have mentioned, a move towards the exaggeration of realistic appearance. This emphasis had two fairly identifiable components that were markedly erotic and related to an extended idea of *inframince* (compared with the abstract idea used in the *Large Glass*). On the one hand, there was the perceptual extension of the visual to include the tactile (while still remaining visual), and on the other hand, and as a result of this, the use of unconventional materials that combined a supra-real quality with the possibility of illustrating *inframince* characteristics. In his notes, Duchamp acknowledges that smells and sounds are better vehicles than visual images for expressing the dimensional interstice implicit in the concept of *inframince* (as we have already seen in practical examples of this principle). Tactility as an aura of visual form — if the right materials are used — overcomes this defect and makes use of the only thing that is capable of capturing the minimal and the multi-dimensional without requiring either prior patterns of configuration or explanatory methods of abstraction: eroticism. Moreover, leather — a sculptural material *par excellence* with supra-real qualities — is, when polished, an alternative to glass, a potential container of *inframince* dimensional extensions, if a dull reflection can be produced on its surface by the use of the right lighting (this possibility appears in Duchamp's notes on *inframince*).

In *Prière de toucher* (*Please Touch*, fig. 113), created for the cover of the catalogue for the 1947 exhibition 'Le Surréalisme en 1947' in Paris, Duchamp produced a foam-rubber breast with a red nipple mounted on black velvet. Both in its execution and in its title, the work is a perfect example of visual tactility. In *Torture-morte* (1959) — a highly realistic foot made of plaster adorned with flies (fig. 124) — the tactile quality is emphasized with irony, as it also is in *Sculpture-morte* (1959), a marzipan sculpture of vegetables devoured by insects (fig. 125). Dating from the same year was the even more mocking work *With my Tongue in my Cheek* — a drawing of the artist's head in profile with a plaster protuberance representing the right cheek deformed by pressure from the tongue inside (fig. 126).

When Duchamp produced *La Boîte-en-valise* (fig. 112) in 1936-41, a Box that was different from the other three already mentioned — or rather their reverse, since it was a portable museum in miniature of his whole œuvre (the others, as we have said, must be considered as protoplastic language) — it could have been taken as a sort of ironic testament, meaning that other works that appeared later were irrelevant. However, in the twenty years from 1946, Duchamp was to labour on something that was as complicated as the *Large Glass* (and closely related to it); and a good number of his works shown during that period were produced in connection with this Installation, which was exhibited only after his death.

Under the title *Esquisse pour 'Étant donnés, le gaz d'éclairage et la chute d'eau'* Duchamp made a drawing in 1944 of the naked figure that was to become the central motif of the work; then, in 1949, the figure was moulded in painted leather on plaster and mounted on velvet (fig. 117). In the same way as with the *Large Glass*, the genesis of the final work involved the production of a series of related pieces that were also valued individually by the artist in his traditional dedication to the process of plastic configuration. Thus, from the moulds of galvanized plaster used for shaping the body of the naked girl, Duchamp produced works of exceptional interest. *Female Fig-leaf* (fig. 119), dating fron 1950, is the mould of the groin; the idea is reminiscent of the *Large Glass*, whilst the title is the reverse of its practical function. In *Wedge of Chastity* (fig. 118), produced in 1954, the galvanized plaster mould (as lubricious as the Bachelor apparatus in the *Large Glass*) interlocks with the soft plastic material; the 'wedge of chastity' is thus hidden

Marcel Duchamp at 5 Rue Parmentier, Neuilly-sur-Seine. 1951. Photograph by Henri Cartier-Bresson.

Teeny and Marcel Duchamp under the awning built by Duchamp at his apartment in Cadaqués.

and with it the *inframince* between the two materials. In *Objet-dard* (fig. 120) of 1951, other territories are invaded; the mould does not enable the form to be identified, and causes a total dilution of conventional meanings, thus producing an interstitial entity (like a hinge). It is a mould for shaping a work — the reverse of the *Large Glass*, which features a set of mould-apparitions; furthermore, as the title phonetically indicates, it is not a Readymade, nor is it a work in itself, though it is an *'objet d'art'*.

Étant donnés: 1. La chute d'eau, 2. Le gaz d'éclairage (fig. 130) (1946-66) contains a good dose of gesture (or insult) in its technical conception, and this is its first link with the *Large Glass*, for both are an intended 'delay' with respect to accumulative and super-technological creation, and a homage to individuality. Both works took a long time to produce and were done in an atmosphere of absolute secrecy and esotericism, far from the presumptuous intellectualizations of the twentieth century. An assemblage of various carefully lit materials, *Étant donnés* . . . is today in the Philadelphia Museum of Art, where it was set up in 1969 by Anne d'Harnoncourt and Paul Matisse in accordance with the instruction manual meticulously compiled by Duchamp himself, who had previously installed the work in his studio. The Installation starts with an old door from a Catalan farmhouse, specially selected for the purpose, which is set in a frame made of bricks from Cadaqués. The massive door has two small holes in it through which the viewer can look if he cares — there is nothing else to guide him. On looking through them, he sees a wall, with a gap in it, separated from the two eye-holes by a camera obscura. Beyond the breach in the wall is a highly realistic tableau. In the foreground, facing the viewer, lies a nude female figure with shaven pubis (the figure is presumed to be based on two well-known works by Courbet, *La Femme au perroquet* and *L'Origine du monde*). The body is partially concealed by dry twigs and its outstretched left hand holds up a gas lamp, while the background consists of a richly painted landscape of thick woods enclosing a pool beneath a waterfall.

The inversion with respect to the *Large Glass* is quite obvious. The subject of the *Large Glass* was stated explicitly in the title (*The Bride Stripped Bare by her Bachelors, Even*) and the work was provided with a guide to viewing contained in the *Green Box*. In *Étant donnés* . . ., on the other hand, everything is visible; the title suggests rather than describes what in the *Large Glass* were conditions, whilst the assembly manual merely gives instructions without attempting to convey any explanation of the content. This manual contains instructions for installing the skeleton framework supporting the appearance, whereas in the *Large Glass* the skeleton of the appearance is the set of images themselves; the negative moulds are thus replaced by the moulded appearance. The 'source' (native) colours become reflection-colours, activated by external lighting.

Continuing the analogies, we see that the eye-holes in the door parallel the 'oculist witnesses' in the *Large Glass*. The Bachelor landscape (of the water wheel) from that work appears as the background of the Installation. The Bride would have fallen into the bushes just at the moment of her expansion which, brightly lit, faces the viewer. The girl would dominate the 'given' conditions of bachelor excitation (desire) — the gaslight and the falling water — and on moving to the bachelor space would have become an appearance. The onanistic mechanisms (the trolley on runners and chocolate grinder) would obviously exist in the mind of the observer.

Nevertheless, this move towards appearance is not a naturalistic, retinal acknowledgment, but a dimensional leap that establishes eroticism as a force in order to produce it. In the Installation, the dimensional excess of the appearance is achieved in several ways. On the one hand, the sky lit internally by a neon tube and executed on unpolished glass gives the background a hazy effect, whilst the waterfall shines weakly. This gloomy, misty background contrasts sharply with the bright lighting on the naked body and, specifically, on its pudenda. Thus the whole takes on the aspect of an ultra-fast snapshot, so that the three-dimensional appearance would be the section through a continuum of greater dimensionality (the fourth dimension, which is not time, for the Installation — like the *Large Glass* — captures an infinitesimal instant). On the other hand, the 'anaglyphic' red and green colouring of the side supports and the upper beam makes the perception of volumes clearer. Finally, the painted leather that forms the skin of the body provides a uniform translucency free of iridescence (as if the surface absorbed the reflection without becoming opaque) highlighting an *inframince* expansion of volume.

The Installation, as a whole, is an inverted projection in a camera obscura, so that the scene is the projection in perspective of the mind of the viewer; hence the emphasizing of the three-dimensional appearance leading towards a territory of greater dimensionality, for through the gap in the wall the viewer 'sees' his insatiable desire for representation inevitably linked to his imagination and knowledge and at the same time strengthened by the perceptual superiority of eroticism (illustrated in the work by the motif and by the tactile sublimation of the materials). The Installation is therefore a tautological celebration in which the spectator is included, as he should be if 'Eros is life' and 'Life is art'. The *Large Glass* is, as we have said, an open-ended work; consequently *Étant donnés...* is too, for the desire for representation is not definable in space (the scene on the other side of the hole cannot be demarcated) and neither is the imagination of the observer, who sees, knows and creates.

Biography

1887. Marcel Duchamp born on 28 July at Blainville-Crevon, near Rouen. His upbringing in a cultured, bourgeois family that was particularly concerned with the arts was to have a considerable influence on both Marcel and his elder brothers Gaston (born 1875) — the painter Jacques Villon — and the sculptor Raymond Duchamp-Villon (born 1876).

1906. Moves to Paris (Montmartre), where he joins his brothers. Publishes cartoons in satirical periodicals.

1910. Exhibits works at the Salon des Indépendants and the Salon d'Automne.
Cartoons published in *Le Courrier Français* and *Le Témoin*. Meets Francis Picabia.

1911. Numerous artists and writers attend the gatherings at Raymond Duchamp-Villon's house in the Paris suburb of Puteaux; in addition to the three Duchamp brothers, others present include Frank Kupka, Albert Gleizes, Fernand Léger, Roger de la Fresnaye and Jean Metzinger.

1912. *Nu descendant un escalier (Nude Descending a Staircase)* is withdrawn by Duchamp after being rejected by the Salon des Indépendants. It is shown, together with *Sonate*, in the Exhibition of Cubist Art at the Galeria Dalmau, Barcelona.
Duchamp, Guillaume Apollinaire and Picabia see a performance of Raymond Roussel's play *Impressions d'Afrique*.
Visit to Munich, July-August.
In October *Nu descendant un escalier* is shown in Paris at the Salon de la Section d'Or, organized by the Puteaux group.
Visits Étival in the Jura mountains in company with Picabia and Apollinaire.
Begins working at the Bibliothèque de Sainte-Geneviève, Paris, where he studies works on perspective.

1913. The Armory Show opens in New York and Duchamp exhibits *The King and Queen Surrounded by Swift Nudes, Portrait of Chess Players, Sad Young Man in a Train* and *Nude Descending a Staircase*. The reviews of the *Nude* bring fame to Duchamp in the United States.
First studies and preparatory notes for *La Mariée mise à nu par ses célibataires, même (Grand Verre)*, the great unfinished work, often called simply the *Large Glass*, that will occupy Duchamp on and off from 1915 to 1923.

1915. Visits New York, where he is invited to the home of Louise and Walter Arensberg, who were to become his friends and patrons and the chief collectors of his works.
Meets Picabia and Gleizes, both recently arrived in the United States.
Introduced to Man Ray.

1916. Meets Beatrice Wood and Henri-Pierre Roché.

1917. Becomes a founder member of the Society of Independent Artists, Inc., of which he is later appointed a director.
For the exhibition of the Independents he submits the Readymade *Fountain*, signed with the pseudonym R. Mutt; its rejection led to the resignations of Duchamp and Arensberg.
With Beatrice Wood and Roché he publishes the reviews *The Blind Man*, of which only two issues were produced, and *Rongwrong*, which had only one issue.

1918. Completes *Tu m'*, his last picture painted on canvas, for Katherine S. Dreier's library in West Redding, Connecticut.
Continues work on drawings for the *Large Glass*.

1919. Visit to Buenos Aires.
Returns to Europe and spends several months in Paris. Attends meetings of the Dada group, attended by André Breton, Tristan Tzara, Paul Éluard and others.

1920. Returns to New York, bringing *50cc of Paris Air* as a gift for Walter Arensberg.
Constructs his first optical machine: *Rotary Glass Plates (Precision Optics)*.
With Katherine S. Dreier and Man Ray creates the Société Anonyme, Inc., the first museum of modern art in the United States.
Creates a female *alter ego* named Rrose Sélavy, subsequently associated with publications of puns and Readymades.

1921. With Man Ray publishes the first and only issue of the review *New York Dada*, in which Duchamp, dressed as Rrose Sélavy, appears on the label of *Belle Haleine, Eau de Voilette*.
Back in Paris, he settles into the apartment belonging to Suzanne and Jean Crotti.
Ownership of the *Large Glass* passes to Katherine S. Dreier when the Arensbergs move to California.

1922. Sails for New York.
Writes to Tristan Tzara suggesting an insignia, as a sort of 'universal panacea', with the four letters DADA.

1923. Decides to leave the *Large Glass* in a state of 'incompletion'.
Visits Brussels for several months to take part in his first major chess tournament, in which he comes third.

1924. He becomes increasingly absorbed by chess and devotes most of his time to it.
Takes part in *Entr'acte*, the film by Picabia and René Clair with music by Erik Satie, in which he appears playing chess with Man Ray.

1925. His mother dies on 29 January, and his father only a few days later, on 3 February.

1926. Completes *Anémic Cinéma* in Paris, filmed with Marc Allegret and Man Ray.
At the 'International Exhibition of Modern Art' organized by the Société Anonyme in the Brooklyn Museum, New York, the *Large Glass* is shown in public for the first time; afterwards, while in transit, the glass panels are broken.
Moves into a rented studio at 11 Rue Larrey.
Sails for New York in October.

1927. Sets up the Brancusi exhibition in Chicago, after having acquired a large number of his sculptures.
Returns to Paris, where he has the two-way *Door* built in his studio.
Marries Lydie Sarazin-Lavassor. The marriage was to last only a few months.

1928. Further chess tournaments. Duchamp is a member of the French Olympic team at The Hague.

1930. In charge of selecting works for the Société Anonyme exhibition to be held in New York the following year. Artists represented include Max Ernst, Joan Miró, Piet Mondrian, and Amédée Ozenfant.

1932. Is appointed a French delegate to the International Chess Federation, and continues as a delegate until 1937.

1933. Takes part in the 'Exposition Surréaliste' at the Galerie Pierre Colle, Paris.
Spends his holidays with Mary Reynolds in Cadaqués, on the Costa Brava, where he gets to know Salvador Dalí and his wife Gala; invites Man Ray to join him.
Sails for New York in October, in order to organize a second Brancusi exhibition.

1934. Returns to Paris. Resumes artistic activities, putting together a selection of preparatory notes, drawings and photos relating to the *Large Glass*; these are published in facsimile in 300 copies as *La Boîte Verte (The Green Box)*.

1935. Becomes captain of the French team for the first chess Olympics by correspondence.
First ideas for *La Boîte-en-valise*, a box that would contain photographs and reproductions of most of his works, issued in a limited edition from 1941.
Takes a stand at the 33rd Concours Lépine (for inventors) in order to exhibit his set of *Rotoreliefs*.

1936. In May returns to the United States.
Various works are selected for several different exhibitions: 'Cubism and Abstract Art' (New York); 'Exposition Surréaliste d'Objets' (Paris); 'International Surrealist Exhibition' (London); 'Fantastic Art, Dada, Surrealism' (New York).

1937. First one-man show, held at the Arts Club of Chicago.
Designs glass door, *Porte Gradiva*, for André Breton's Paris gallery.

1938. Sets up the 'Exposition Internationale du Surréalisme' in Paris, in collaboration with Breton, Éluard and others.
In London participates in selection of contemporary sculpture for summer exhibition at Guggenheim Jeune.

1939. *Rrose Sélavy, oculisme de précision, poils et coups de pieds en tous genres*, a collection of puns, is published in Paris.

1942. Sails from Lisbon for New York. Stays for a while with Max Ernst. With André Breton and others, organizes the exhibition 'First Papers of Surrealism', for which he designs the installation, using a 'mile of string'.

1943. Moves into studio at 210 West 14th Street.
Together with Breton and Kurt Seligmann, designs the window display for Brentano's bookshop on Fifth Avenue on the occasion of the publication of *La Part du diable* by Denis de Rougemont.
Designs the cover of issue 2-3 of the review *VVV*, of which he, Ernst and Breton form the panel of editors.

1945. Designs the cover of the March issue of *View*, which is devoted to his work.
With Enrico Donati, designs window displays for Brentano's on the occasion of the publication of Breton's *Arcane 17* and the second edition of *Le Surréalisme et la peinture*.

1946. Starts work on the installation *Étant donnés . . .*, on which he would work secretly in his studio for over twenty years and which was shown in public only after his death.
Takes part in a film (begun in 1944) by Hans Richter entitled *Dreams that Money Can Buy* (with music by John Cage), in which Alexander Calder, Max Ernst, Fernand Léger and Man Ray also participate.
Produces *Prière de toucher* for the cover of the de luxe edition of 'Le Surréalisme en 1947' at the Galerie Maeght, Paris.

1949. Travels to San Francisco to take part in a three-day debate on modern art; among those attending are Robert Goldwater, Darius Milhaud, Arnold Schoenberg, Mark Tobey and Frank Lloyd Wright.
Visits the exhibition 'Twentieth Century Art from the Louise and Walter Arensberg Collection' (including thirty works by Duchamp), held at the Art Institute of Chicago.

1950. The catalogue *Collection of the Société Anonyme* (Yale University Art Gallery) includes thirty-three critical studies of artists written by Duchamp between 1943 and 1949.
The Arensbergs decide to donate their art collection to the Philadelphia Museum of Art.

1952. Takes part in the filming of Hans Richter's *8 × 8*.

1953. Collaborates in the organization of the exhibition 'Dada 1916-1923' in New York, which includes twelve of his works.
Produces a poster-catalogue printed on tissue paper.
The exhibition 'Marcel Duchamp, Francis Picabia' in New York includes five works by Duchamp.

1954. Marries Alexina (Teeny) Sattler in New York on 16 January; they live in an apartment at 327 East 58th Street until 1959.
The *Large Glass* (bequeathed by Katherine Dreier) is installed permanently in the Philadelphia Museum of Art, together with the Louise and Walter Arensberg Collection (which includes forty-seven works by Duchamp).

1955. Acquires United States citizenship; his witnesses are Alfred Barr (Director of The Museum of Modern Art), James Johnson Sweeney (of the Solomon R. Guggenheim Museum) and James Thrall Sobey (of Yale University Art Gallery).

1956. Is included in the 'Dada' (Yale) and 'Cubism 1910-1912' (New York) exhibitions.

1957. A joint exhibition 'Jacques Villon, Raymond Duchamp-Villon, Marcel Duchamp' opens in New York at the Guggenheim Museum.

1958. '50 Ans d'Art Moderne' at the Brussels International Exposition includes works by Duchamp.
Spends August in Cadaqués; from now onwards he was to spend many summers there.

1959. Robert Lebel's book *Sur Marcel Duchamp*, the first general monograph on Duchamp, is published in Paris.
Duchamp settles in an apartment at 28 West 10th Street, New York, where he and Teeny will live from now on.
Takes part in the 'Exposition Internationale du Surréalisme' organized by André Breton in Paris, which is devoted to eroticism.

1960. Many artists of the new generation, such as Richard Hamilton, Robert Rauschenberg, Jasper Johns, Robert Morris, Arman, Ben, etc., show an interest in Duchamp's work. He follows certain aspects of the contemporary art scene closely — e.g. Claes Oldenburg's Happenings and Jean Tinguely's self-destructing *Hommage à New York*.
Is elected a member of the National Institute of Arts and Letters, New York.

1961. Participates in an exhibition 'Art in Motion' organized by the Stedelijk Museum in Amsterdam and the Moderna Museet in Stockholm. Replicas of some of his works are produced for the occasion, notably the *Large Glass*, by Ulf Linde.

Honorary degree of Doctor of Humanities conferred by Wayne State University, Detroit.
A doctoral thesis on his work is completed by Lawrence D. Steefel, Jr at Princeton University.

1963. Visits California to attend the opening of the first major retrospective exhibition of his works, entitled 'By or of Marcel Duchamp or Rrose Sélavy', at the Pasadena Art Museum.
Gives lecture entitled 'Apropos of Myself' at the Baltimore Museum of Art and at Brandeis University, Waltham, Massachusetts.

1964. Arturo Schwarz produces replicas of thirteen Readymades in sets of 8, and organizes the one-man show 'Omaggio a Marcel Duchamp' at his gallery in Milan.

1965. Helps to organize the exhibition 'Not Seen and/or Less Seen of/by Marcel Duchamp/Rrose Sélavy 1904-1964' in New York, which includes ninety works from the Mary Sisler Collection. The invitation features a Readymade *Mona Lisa* printed on a playing card.
In Paris, the Association pour l'Étude du Mouvement Dada, whose president was Michel Sanouillet, organizes a dinner in honour of Rrose Sélavy, Duchamp attends, and as Rrose Sélavy signs an urn containing the ash from his after-dinner cigar.

1966. Attends the opening in London of 'The Almost Complete Works of Marcel Duchamp' at the Tate Gallery, the first major retrospective exhibition of his works held in Europe, including 242 items and the second replica of the *Large Glass*, this one produced by the organizer of the exhibition for the Arts Council of Great Britain, Richard Hamilton.
The special July issue of the review *Art and Artists* is devoted to Marcel Duchamp.
Completes *Étant donnés: 1. La chute d'eau, 2. Le gaz d'éclairage*, begun in 1946.

1967. Attends the International Chess Tournament in Monte Carlo. Collaborates in setting up the exhibition 'Les Duchamp: Jacques Villon, Raymond Duchamp-Villon, Marcel Duchamp, Suzanne Duchamp' in Rouen. Part of the exhibition (the works of Raymond and Marcel) is later shown at the Musée National d'Art Moderne, Paris, Duchamp's first large show in the French capital. Publishes a limited edition of *À l'Infinitif (La Boîte Blanche)*, in New York, which contains 79 notes and preliminary studies for the *Large Glass*.
Drafts the notes and accompanying photographs for assembling *Etant donnés . . .*, which would finally be installed in the Philadelphia Museum of Art in 1969.

1968. In Toronto, takes part in 'Reunion' a musical performance staged by John Cage, involving a game of chess played by Cage, Marcel and Teeny.
Attends the Second Buffalo Festival of the Arts for the premiere of the ballet *Walkaround Time* by Merce Cunningham, with sets inspired by the *Large Glass* and constructed under the supervision of Jasper Johns.
In New York attends the opening on 27 March of 'Dada, Surrealism and their Heritage', an exhibition (containing a dozen of his works) organized by William S. Rubin at The Museum of Modern Art.
Travels to Monte Carlo to attend the International Chess Tournament.
In May leaves Paris on a trip to Switzerland and Italy, and then sails from Genoa to Barcelona.
Stays in Cadaqués, where he works on the fireplace and chimney anaglyph, 'Cheminée anaglyphe', that he intended to install in his apartment there.
Returns to Paris in the autumn; dies suddenly in Neuilly on 2 October.
He is buried in the cemetery in Rouen; the epitaph on the gravestone, written by himself, reads: 'D'ailleurs c'est toujours les autres qui meurent' (But it's always other people who die).

Select Bibliography

A. WRITINGS BY MARCEL DUCHAMP

Boîte de 1914 (manuscript notes, 1 drawing; original and 3 photocopies). 1914.

L'Opposition et les cases conjuguées sont réconciliées (in collaboration with V. Halberstadt), Edition de L'Echiquier, Paris and Brussels, 1932.

'La mariée mise à nu par ses célibataires, même'. *Le Surréalisme au Service de la Révolution* (Paris), no. 5, May 1933, pp. 1-2.

La Mariée mise à nu par ses célibataires, même (La Boîte Verte) (94 documents; facsimiles of manuscripts, drawings and photographs, in a box; standard edition of 300), Édition Rrose Sélavy, Paris, 1934.

Rrose Sélavy (Oculisme de précision . . .; a volume of puns), Éditions G.L.M., Paris, 1939.

In catalogue *Collection of the Société Anonyme; Museum of Modern Art 1920*, thirty-three brief critical reviews of contemporary artists. Yale University Art Gallery, for Associates in Fine Arts, New Haven, Conn., 1950.

'Une lettre de Marcel Duchamp' (to André Breton), *Medium* (Paris), n.s., no. 4, January 1955, p. 33.

'The Creative Act', text of lecture reprinted in *Art News* (New York), vol. 56, no. 4, Summer 1957.

Lettre de Marcel Duchamp (1921) à Tristan Tzara, P.A.B., Alès (Gard), 1958.

Marchand du sel (writings of Marcel Duchamp edited by Michel Sanouillet), Le Terrain Vague, Paris, 1958. English edition, *Salt Seller. The Writings of Marcel Duchamp (Marchand du Sel)*, Oxford University

Press, New York, 1973; also published as *The Essential Writings of Marcel Duchamp*, Thames and Hudson, London, 1975.

À l'Infinitif (unpublished notes, 1912-20, mostly for the *Large Glass*), de luxe edition of 150 copies known as *The White Box/La Boîte blanche* (with English translation by Cleve Gray), Cordier & Ekstrom, New York, 1967.

Duchamp du Signe (revised and enlarged edition of *Marchand du sel* 1958), Flammarion, Paris, 1975.

Marcel Duchamp, notes (manuscript notes in facsimile and transcription — in French and English; preface by Pontus Hultén; introduction and English translation by Paul Matisse), Centre National d'Art et de Culture Georges Pompidou, Paris, 1980.

Marcel Duchamp. Die Schriften (German translation and comments by Serge Stauffer), Regenbogen Verlag, Zurich, 1981.

Manual of Instructions for Étant Donnés: 1. La chute d'eau, 2. Le gaz d'éclairage. Philadelphia Museum of Art, Philadelphia, 1987.

Lettres de Marcel Duchamp à Marcel Jean, Verlag Silke Schreiber, Munich, 1988 (trilingual edition).

B. SPECIAL ISSUES OF PERIODICALS AND REVIEWS

View (New York), vol. 5, no. 1, March 1945. Articles by Breton, Buffet, Calas, Desnos and others; cover by Duchamp.

Art and Artists (London), vol. 1, no. 4, July 1966. Articles by Otto Hahn, André Breton, Robert Lebel, Brian O'Doherty, Richard Hamilton, George Heard Hamilton, Alexander Watt, Simon Watson Taylor, Toby Mussmanly, Christopher Finch; cover by Duchamp.

Philadelphia Museum of Art Bulletin, vol. 64, no. 299-300, April-September 1969. Articles by Evan H. Turner, Anne d'Harnoncourt and Walter Hopps; new edition, revised and enlarged, 1987.

Art in America (New York), vol. 57, no. 4, July-August 1969. Articles by Cleve Gray, Walter Hopps, Alexander Calder, Jasper Johns, Nicolas Calas, William Copley and Hans Richter. Interviews by Dorothy Norman and Colette Roberts.

Opus International (Paris), no. 49, March 1974. Articles by Alain Jouffroy, Man Ray, Arturo Schwarz, Robert Cordier, Jindrich Chalupecký, Kim Levin, Nicolas Calas, Allan Kaprow, Michael Kirby, Octavio Paz, Jean-Clarence Lambert, Alain Roussel, Ben, Gérard Durozoi, Gérald Gassiot-Talabot, Gilles Aillaud, Eduardo Arroyo, Antonio Recalcati, Michel Troche and Enrico Crispoldi. Interviews with John Cage and Daniel Pommereulle by Alain Jouffroy.

L'Arc (Aix-en-Provence), no. 59, 4, 1974. Articles by Jean Clair, Gilbert Lascault, Marc Le Bot, Bernard Pingaud, Roger Dadoun, Arturo Schwarz, Jean Suquet, Georges Raillard, René Micha, Bernard Teyssèdre, Daniel Charles, Harald Szeeman and Ben.

Studio International (London), vol. 189, no. 973, January-February 1975. Supplement devoted to Marcel Duchamp (pp. 19-60), with articles by Anthony Hill, Max Bill, Jindrich Chalupecký, Margit Rowell and Katrina Martin. Interview with François Le Lyonnais by Ralf Rumney.

El Urogallo (Madrid), nos. 15, 16, 17, July, August, September 1987. Articles by Antoni Tàpies, José Jiménez, Gloria Moure, Chema Cobo, José Luis Brea.

La Vanguardia (Barcelona), Tuesday, 28 July 1987: weekly supplement on culture devoted to Marcel Duchamp. Articles by John Cage, José Jiménez, Félix Fanes, Miquel Tàpies, Jasper Johns, Otto Hahn, Ignasi de Solà-Morales and Gloria Moure.

C. MONOGRAPHS, CATALOGUES AND INTERVIEWS

ADCOCK, Craig Elmo: *Marcel Duchamp's notes for 'La Mariée mise à nu par ses célibataires, même'*, UMI Research Press, Ann Arbor, Michigan, 1983.

CABANNE, Pierre: *Entretiens avec Marcel Duchamp*, Pierre Belfond, Paris, 1967; English translation, *Dialogues with Marcel Duchamp* (Documents of 20th Century Art), Thames and Hudson, London, and Viking Press, New York, 1971.

CALVESI, Maurizio: *Duchamp invisible*, Officina, Rome, 1975.

CLAIR, Jean: *Duchamp ou le grand fictif: essai de mythanalyse du Grand verre*, Galilée, Paris, 1975.

CLAIR, Jean: *L'Œuvre de Marcel Duchamp*, with texts by Ulf Linde, Jean-François Lyotard, Robert Lebel *et al.*, Musée National d'Art Moderne, Centre National d'Art et de Culture Georges Pompidou, Paris, 1977. Catalogue of the retrospective exhibition.

D'HARNONCOURT, Anne and McSHINE, Kynaston (eds.): exhibition catalogue *Marcel Duchamp*, with texts by Michel Sanouillet, Richard Hamilton, Arturo Schwarz *et al.*, The Museum of Modern Art, New York, and the Philadelphia Museum of Art, 1973, and Thames and Hudson, London, 1974.

DE DUVE, Thierry: *Nominalisme Pictural. Marcel Duchamp, la Peinture et la Modernité*, Les Éditions de Minuit, Paris, 1984.

LEBEL, Robert: *Sur Marcel Duchamp*, Trianon Press, Paris, 1959; English translation, *Marcel Duchamp*, Grove Press, New York, 1959; new edition, Grossman Publishers, New York, 1967.

LYOTARD, Jean-François: *Les Transformateurs Duchamp*, Galilée, Paris, 1977.

MOURE, Gloria: *Duchamp*, with texts by John Cage, Octavio Paz, Dawn Ades, Yoshiaki Tono, Germano Celant *et al.*, Caja de Pensiones, Barcelona, 1984. Catalogue of retrospective exhibition.

PAZ, Octavio: *Marcel Duchamp*, Ediciones Era, Mexico City, 1968.

PAZ, Octavio: *Apariencia desnuda. La obra de Marcel Duchamp*, Ediciones Era, Mexico City, 1973; second, revised and enlarged edition 1978. French translation by Monique Fong-Wust: *L'apparence mise à nu . . .*, Gallimard, Paris, 1977.

SCHWARZ, Arturo. *The Complete Works of Marcel Duchamp*, Thames and Hudson, London, and Harry N. Abrams, New York, 1969; second, revised edition 1970.

SCHWARZ, Arturo: *The Alchemist Stripped Bare in the Bachelor, Even*, The Museum of Modern Art, New York, 1973.

STAUFFER, Serge: *Marcel Duchamp . . . ready-made!*, Regenbogen Verlag, Zurich, 1973.

SUQUET, Jean: *Miroir de la mariée*, Flammarion, Paris, 1974.

SUQUET, Jean: *Le Guéridon et la virgule*, Christian Bourgeois, Paris, 1976.

1. *Yvonne*, 1902.
   Indian ink, pencil and watercolour on paper, 38.5 × 28.5 cm.
   Private collection, Paris.

2. *Church at Blainville*, 1902.
   Oil on canvas, 61×42.5 cm.
   Philadelphia Museum of Art,
   The Louise and Walter Arensberg Collection.

3. *Yvonne (in kimono)*, 1901.
   Ink, pencil and watercolour on paper, 29.5×22 cm.
   Private collection, Paris.

4. *Play?* 1902.
   Indian ink on paper, 20.5×15.5 cm.
   Private collection, Paris.

2

3

4

5. *Suzanne Duchamp Seated*, 1903.
   Coloured pencils on paper, 49.5×32 cm.
   Private collection, Paris.

6. *Portrait of Jacques Villon*, 1904-05.
   Charcoal drawing on double sheet of paper, 31×20.2 cm.
   Collection Dr Robert Jullien, Paris.

7. *Parva Domus, Magna Quies*, 1902.
   Indian ink on paper, 16×20.5 cm.
   Private collection, Paris.

8. *For the Menu of Simone Delacour's First Communion Dinner*, 1909.
   Etching and watercolour on paper, 21.5×25 cm.
   Private collection, Paris.

5

6

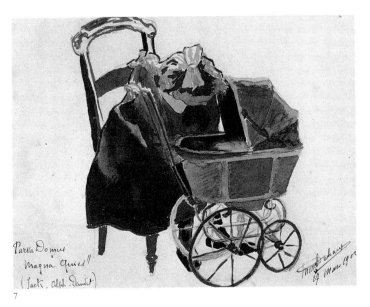

7

8

9. *Portrait of Yvonne Duchamp*, 1909.
    Oil on canvas, 86.5×67.3 cm.
    The Mary Sisler Collection; courtesy, Fourcade, Droll, Inc.,
    New York.

10. *Man Seated by a Window*, 1907.
    Oil on canvas, 55.6×38.7 cm.
    The Mary Sisler Collection; courtesy, Fourcade, Droll, Inc.,
    New York.

11. *Two Nudes*, 1910.
    Oil on canvas, 71.5×91 cm.
    Musée National d'Art Moderne, Paris.

12. *Nude with Black Stockings*, 1910.
    Oil on canvas, 116×89 cm.
    Collection Mr and Mrs Marcos Micha, Mexico City.

11

13

14

13. *The Chess Game*, 1910.
Oil on canvas, 114 × 146 cm.
Philadelphia Museum of Art,
The Louise and Walter Arensberg Collection.

14. *Laundry-barge*, 1910.
Oil on cardboard 66 × 74 cm.
The Mary Sisler Collection; courtesy, Fourcade, Droll, Inc.,
New York.

15. *Portrait of the Artist's Father*, 1910.
Oil on canvas, 92 × 73 cm.
Philadelphia Museum of Art,
The Louise and Walter Arensberg Collection.

16. *Portrait of Dr Dumouchel*, 1910.
    Oil on canvas, 100 × 65 cm.
    Philadelphia Museum of Art,
    The Louise and Walter Arensberg Collection.

17. *Portrait bust of Chauvel*, 1910.
    Oil on cardboard, 55 × 41 cm.
    Private collection, Paris.

18. *Portrait of Dr Ferdinand Tribout*, 1910.
    Oil on canvas, 55 × 45 cm.
    Musée des Beaux-Arts, Rouen

17

18

19. *Standing Nude*, 1910.
    Gouache on cardboard, 60×38 cm.
    Musée des Beaux-Arts, Rouen

20. *The Bush*, 1910-11.
    Oil on canvas, 127×92 cm.
    Philadelphia Museum of Art,
    The Louise and Walter Arensberg Collection.

21. *Baptism*, 1911.
Oil on canvas, 91.7 × 72.7 cm.
Philadelphia Museum of Art,
The Louise and Walter Arensberg Collection.

22. *Nude on Nude*, 1910-11.
Oil on cardboard, 65 × 50 cm.
Collection Julie Hollanda Fawcus, Paris.

23

24

23. *Draught on the Japanese Apple Tree*, 1911.
    Oil on canvas, 61 × 50 cm.
    Collection Dr S. H. Jurmand, Paris

24. *Paradise*, 1910-11.
    Oil on canvas, 114.5 × 128.5 cm.
    Philadelphia Museum of Art,
    The Louise and Walter Arensberg Collection.

25. *Landscape*, 1911.
    Oil on canvas, 46.3 × 61.3 cm.
    The Museum of Modern Art, New York,
    Katherine S. Dreier Bequest, 1953.

25

26. *Apropos of Little Sister*, 1911.
    Oil on canvas, 73 × 60 cm.
    Solomon R. Guggenheim Museum, New York.

27. *Yvonne and Magdeleine in Tatters*, 1911.
    Oil on canvas, 60 × 73 cm.
    Philadelphia Museum of Art,
    The Louise and Walter Arensberg Collection.

27

28. *Sonata*, 1911.
    Oil on canvas, 145 × 113 cm.
    Philadelphia Museum of Art,
    The Louise and Walter Arensberg Collection.

29. *Dulcinea*, 1911.
    Oil on canvas, 146 × 114 cm.
    Philadelphia Museum of Art,
    The Louise and Walter Arensberg Collection.

30. *Mediocrity*, 1911.
    Pencil on paper, 16.5 × 20 cm.
    Private collection, Paris.

31. *Study for 'Portrait of Chess Players'*, 1911.
    Charcoal on paper, 49.5 × 50.5 cm.
    Private collection, New York.

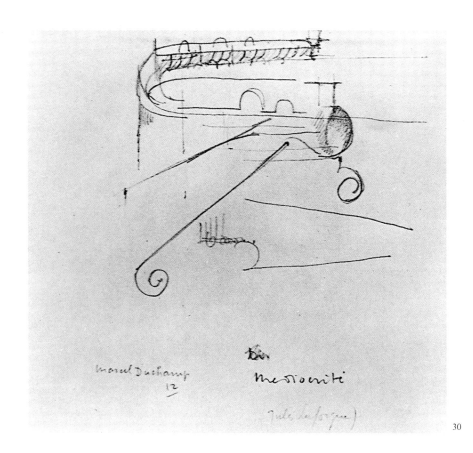

30

31

32. *The Chess Players*, 1911.
    Oil on canvas, 50×61 cm.
    Musée National d'Art Moderne, Paris.

33. *Study for 'Portrait of Chess Players'*, 1911.
Charcoal on paper, 43.1 × 58.4 cm.
Private collection, Paris.

34. *Study for 'Portrait of Chess Players'* or
For a Game of Chess, 1911.
Indian ink and charcoal on paper, 45 × 61.5 cm.
Private collection, Paris.

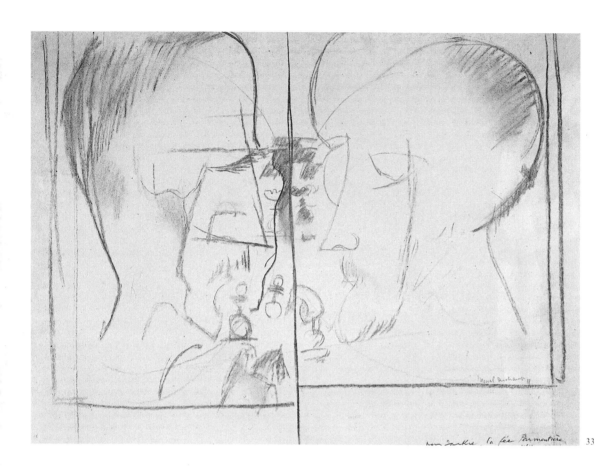

33

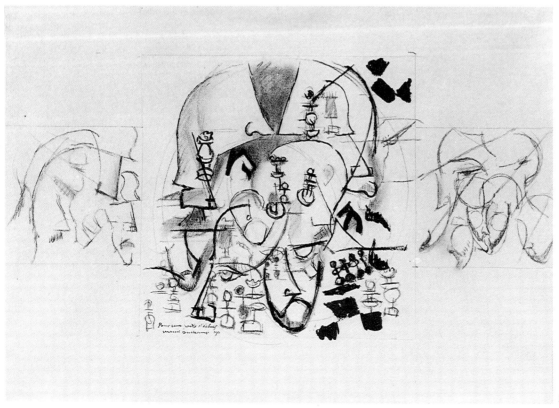

35. *Portrait of Chess Players*, 1911.
    Oil on canvas, 108×101 cm.
    Philadelphia Museum of Art,
    The Louise and Walter Arensberg Collection.

36. *Coffee Mill*, 1911.
    Ink on paper, 20.5 × 14 cm.
    Private collection, Paris.

37. *Coffee Mill*, 1911.
    Oil on cardboard, 33 × 12.5 cm.
    Tate Gallery, London.

37

38. *Young Man and Girl in Spring*, 1911.
    Oil on canvas, 65.7 × 50.2 cm.
    Collection Arturo Schwarz, Milan.

39. *Sad Young Man in a Train*, 1911.
    Oil on canvas mounted on cardboard, 100 × 73 cm.
    Peggy Guggenheim Foundation, Venice.

40

41

40. *Nude on a Ladder*, 1907-08.
    Pencil on paper, 29.5 × 21.5 cm.
    Collection Dr Robert Jullien, Paris.

41. *Nude on a Ladder*, 1907-08.
    Pencil on paper, 29.5 × 21.5 cm.
    Private collection, Paris.

42. *Nude Descending a Staircase, No. 2*, 1912.
    Oil on canvas, 146 × 89 cm.
    Philadelphia Museum of Art,
    The Louise and Walter Arensberg Collection.

43. *Portrait of Gustave Candel's Mother*, 1911-12.
Oil on canvas, 61 × 43.5 cm.
Yoland Candel Collection, Paris.

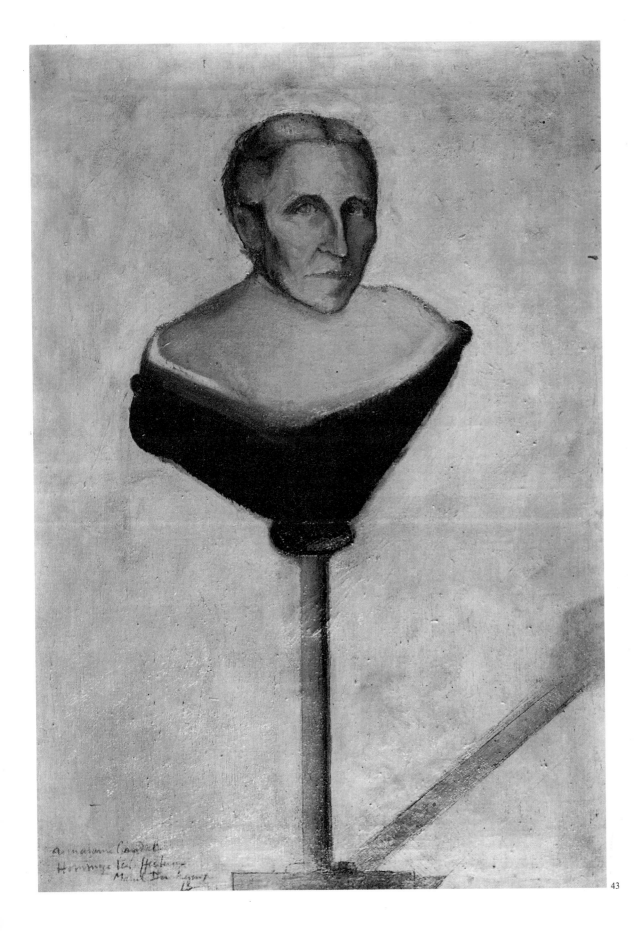

44. *Two Nudes: One Strong and One Swift*, 1912.
Pencil on paper, 30 × 36 cm.
Private collection, Paris.

45. *Two Personages and a Car (Study)*, 1912.
Charcoal on paper, 35 × 29 cm.
Private collection, Paris.

44

45

46. *The King and Queen Traversed by Swift Nudes*, 1912.
Pencil on paper, 27.3 × 39 cm.
Philadelphia Museum of Art,
The Louise and Walter Arensberg Collection.

47. *The Bride Stripped Bare by the Bachelors*, 1912.
Pencil and wash on paper, 23.8 × 32.1 cm.
Musée National d'Art Moderne, Paris.

46

47

48. *The King and Queen Traversed by Nudes at High Speed*, 1912.
Watercolour and gouache on paper, 48.9 × 59.1 cm.
Philadelphia Museum of Art,
The Louise and Walter Arensberg Collection.

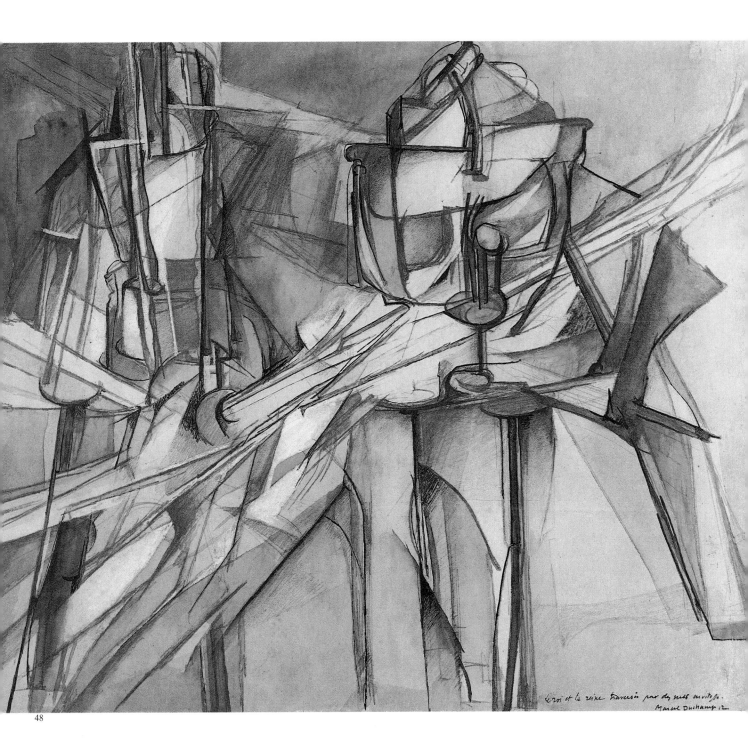

49. *The King and Queen Surrounded by Swift Nudes*, 1912.
Oil on canvas, 114.5×128.5 cm.
Philadelphia Museum of Art,
The Louise and Walter Arensberg Collection.

50. *The Passage from Virgin to Bride*, 1912.
Oil on canvas, 59.4×54 cm.
The Museum of Modern Art, New York.

49

LE PASSAGE de la vierge à la mariée   MARCEL DUCHAMP

51. *Virgin, No. 1*, 1912.
   Pencil on paper, 33.6×25.2 cm.
   Philadelphia Museum of Art,
   A.E. Gallatin Collection.

52. *Virgin, No. 2*, 1912.
   Watercolour and pencil on paper, 40×25.7 cm.
   Philadelphia Museum of Art,
   The Louise and Walter Arensberg Collection.

53. *Bride*, 1912.
   Oil on canvas, 89.5×55 cm.
   Philadelphia Museum of Art,
   The Louise and Walter Arensberg Collection.

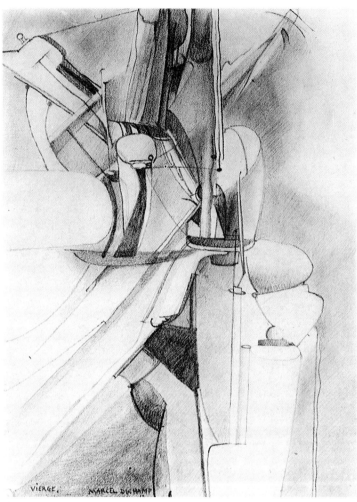

51

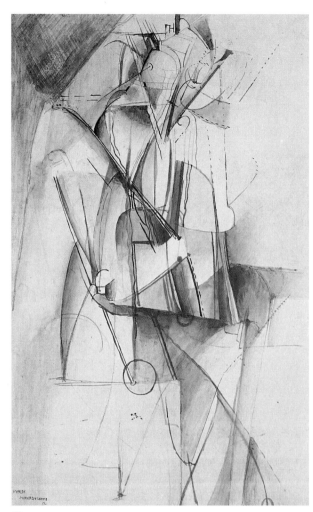

52

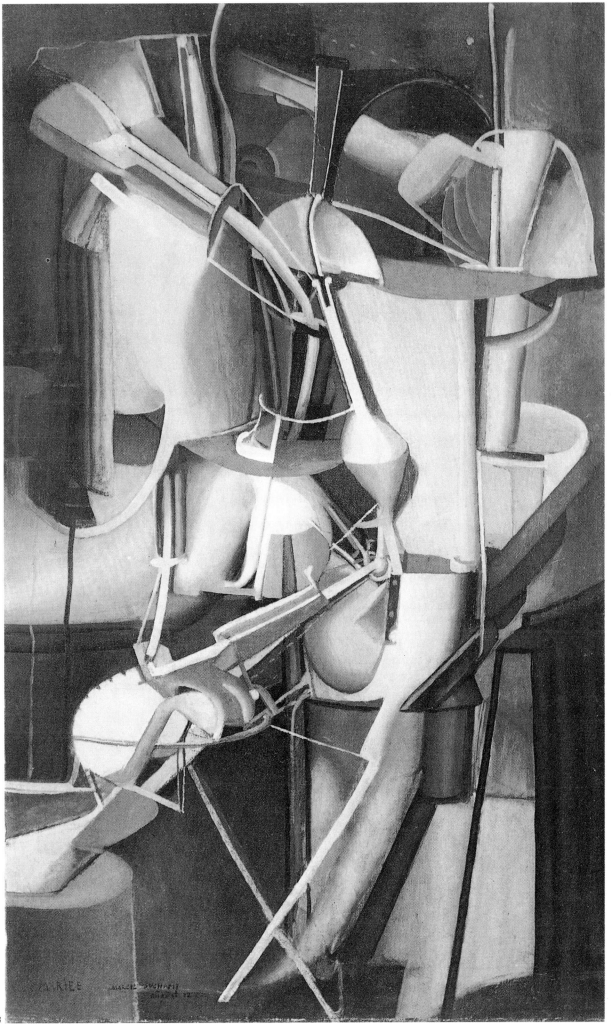

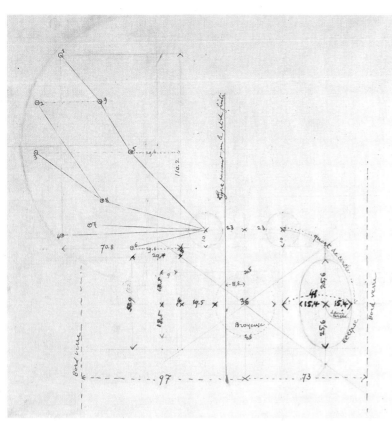

54

54. *Bachelor Apparatus (plan)*, 1913.
Black and red ink on paper, 23×23 cm.
Private collection, Paris.

55. *Bachelor Apparatus (elevation)*, 1913.
Black and red ink on paper, 24×17 cm.
Private collection, Paris.

56. *Boxing Match*, 1913.
Pencil and crayon on paper, 42×31 cm.
Philadelphia Art Museum of Art,
The Louise and Walter Arensberg Collection.

57. *The Bride Stripped Bare by her Bachelors, Even*, 1913.
Pencil on tracing paper, 33×28 cm.
Private collection, Paris.

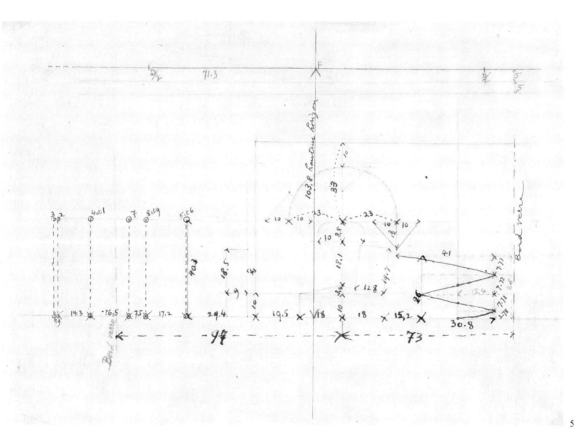

55

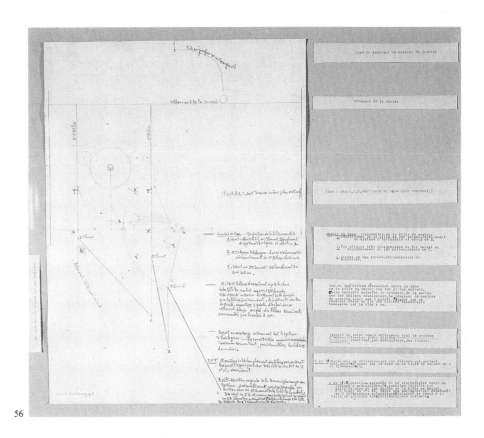

56

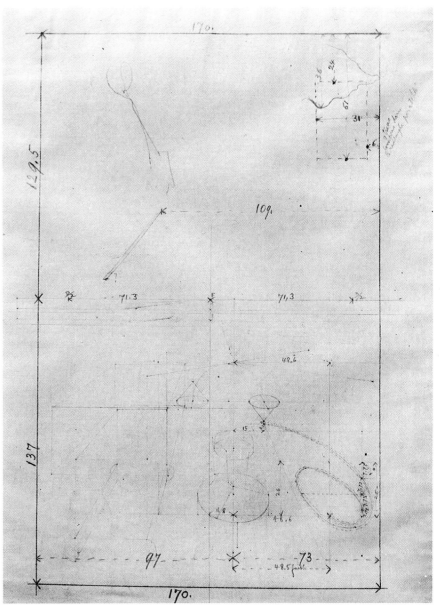

57

58. *Cemetery of Uniforms and Liveries, No. 1*, 1913.
Pencil on paper, 32×40.5 cm.
Philadelphia Museum of Art,
The Louise and Walter Arensberg Collection.

59. *The Knife-grinder*, 1904-05.
Pencil and Indian ink on paper, 21×13 cm.
Private collection, Paris.

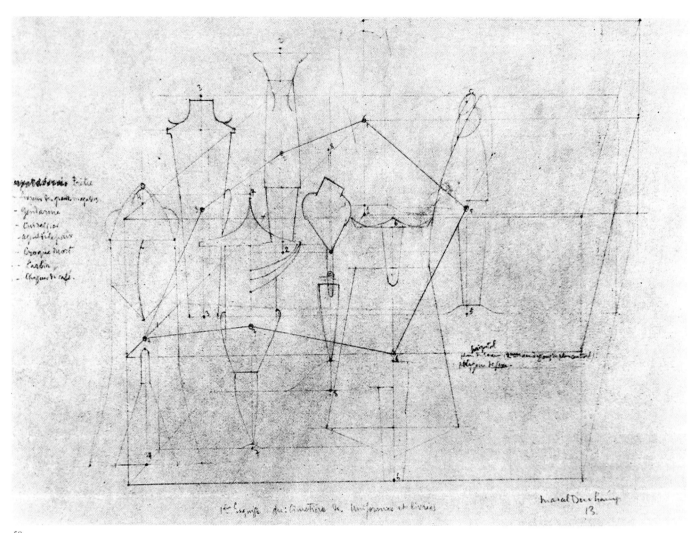

58

59

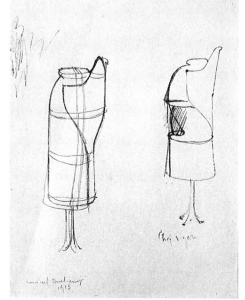

60

60. *Studies for the Bachelors: Station-master*, 1913.
    One side of double-sided drawing, pencil on paper, 21.3 × 16.5 cm.
    Private collection, New York.

61. *Nine Malic Moulds*, 1914-15.
    Oil paint, lead wire and sheet lead on glass (cracked in 1916),
    mounted between two glass plates, 66 × 101.2 cm.
    Private collection, Paris.

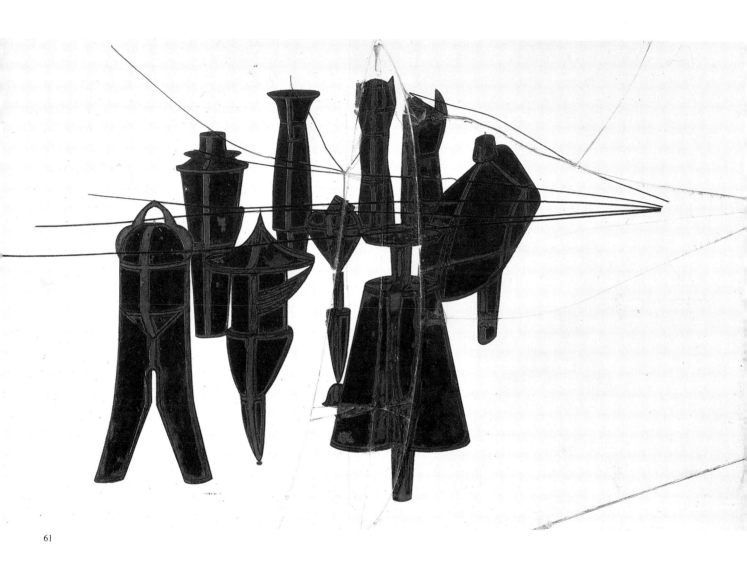

61

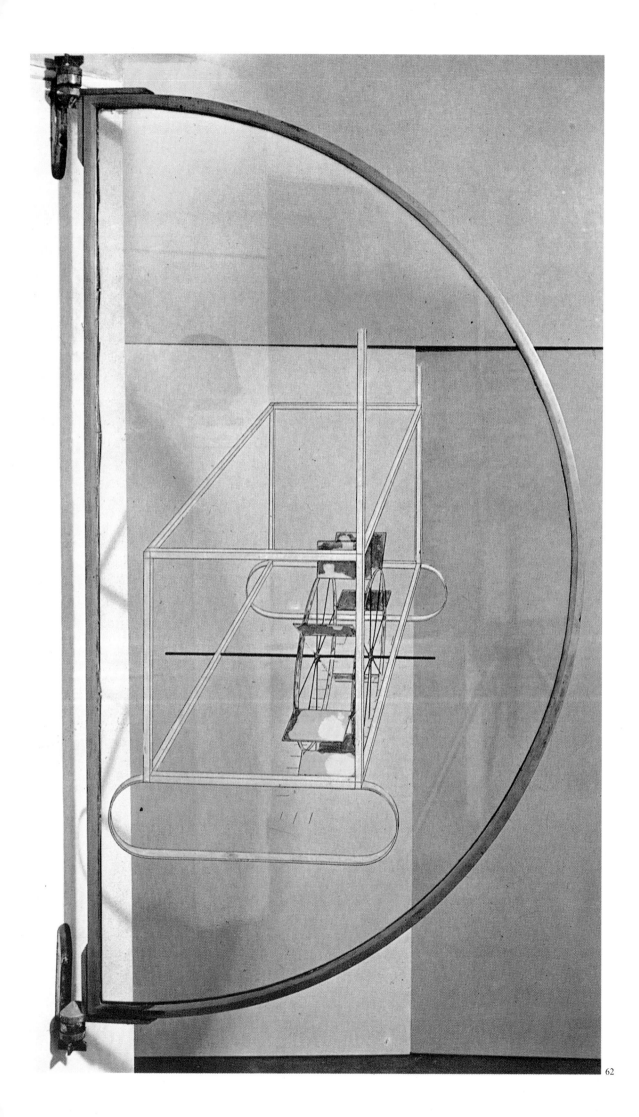

62. *Glider Containing a Water Mill in Neighbouring Metals*, 1913-15.
Oil paint and lead wire on a semicircular sheet of glass, 147 × 79 cm.
Philadelphia Museum of Art,
The Louise and Walter Arensberg Collection.

63. *Musical Erratum*, 1913.
Ink on music paper, 32 × 48 cm.
Private collection, Paris.

64. *Perspective Drawing for the Water-mill Wheel*, 1913 [cf. fig. 62].
Pencil on paper, 30.5 × 19.7 cm.
Private collection, New York.

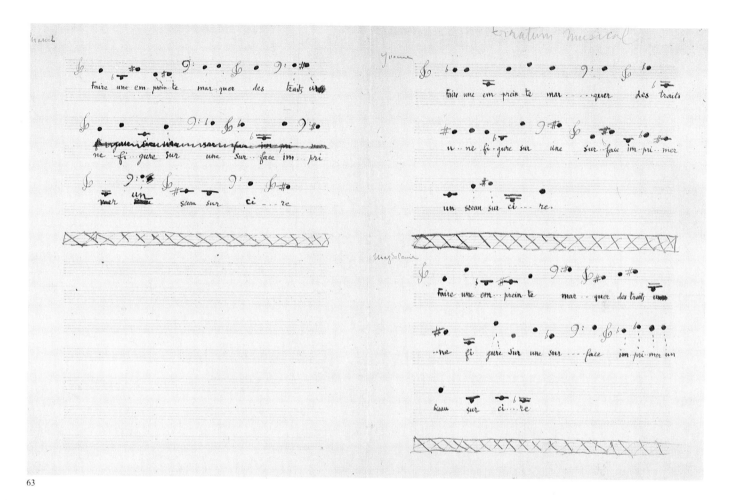

63

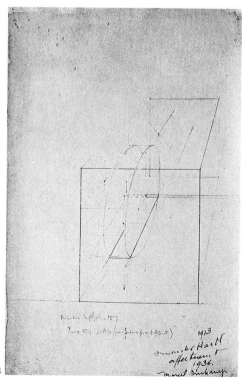

64

65. *Bicycle Wheel*, 1913 (replica 1964; original lost).
Readymade: bicycle wheel (diameter 64.8 cm) fixed to a stool (60.2 cm high).
Private collection, Milan.

66. *The Box of 1914*, 1913-14.
Facsimiles of 16 manuscript notes and a drawing, mounted on 15 boards, each 25 × 18.5 cm, contained in a cardboard box.
Philadelphia Museum of Art,
by courtesy of Mme Marcel Duchamp.

67. *Pharmacy*, 1914.
Rectified Readymade: gouache on a commercial print, 26.2 × 19.2 cm.
Private collection, New York.

68. *To Have the Apprentice in the Sun*, 1914.
Indian ink and pencil on music paper, 27.3 × 17.2 cm.
Philadelphia Museum of Art,
The Louise and Walter Arensberg Collection.

66

67

68

69. *Study for the 'Chocolate Grinder, No. 2',* , 1914.
    Oil paint and pencil on canvas, 73 × 60 cm.
    Kunstsammlung Nordrhein-Westfalen, Düsseldorf.

70. *Chocolate Grinder, No. 2*, 1914.
    Oil paint, thread and lead pencil on canvas, 65 × 54 cm.
    Philadelphia Museum of Art,
    The Louise and Walter Arensberg Collection.

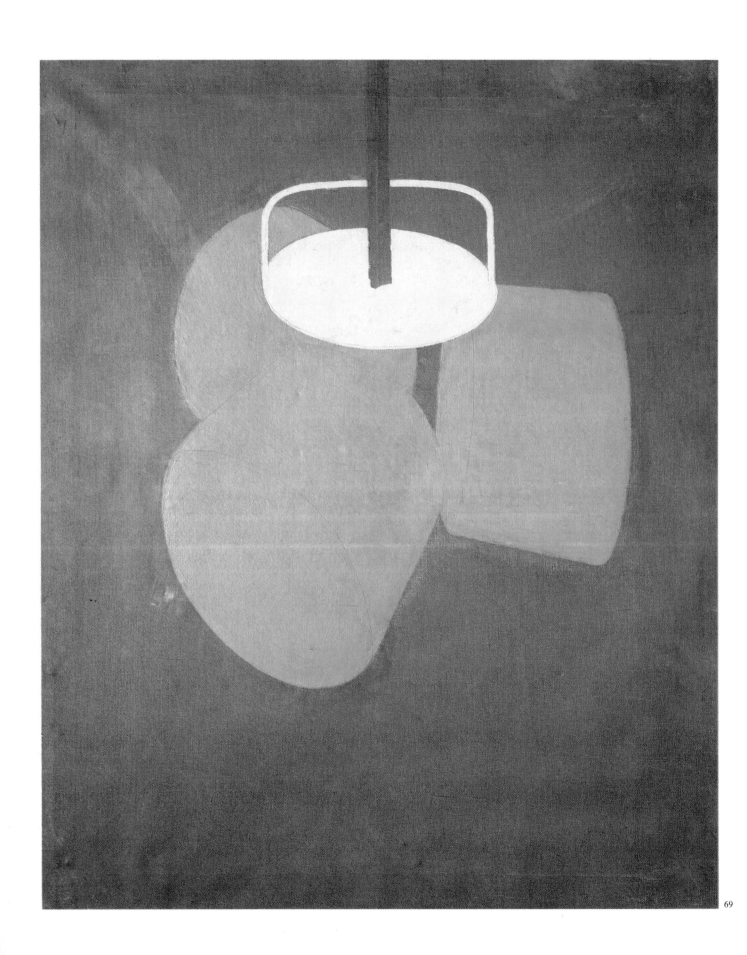

BROYEUSE DE CHOCOLAT · 1914

71. *Réseaux des stoppages (Network of Stoppages)*, 1914.
    Oil and pencil on canvas, 148.9 × 197.7 cm.
    The Museum of Modern Art, New York.
    Abby Aldrich Rockefeller Fund and Gift of Mrs William
    Sisler, 1970.

72. *Draught Piston*, 1914.
    Photograph, 58.8 × 50 cm.
    Private collection, Paris.

73. *First Study for the Sieves*, 1914.
    Pencil on tracing paper, 28.7 × 21.4 cm.
    Private collection, Paris.

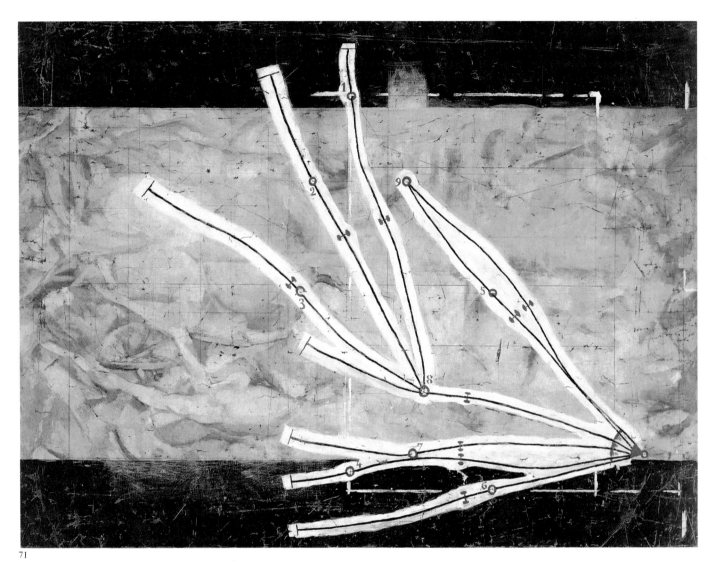

71

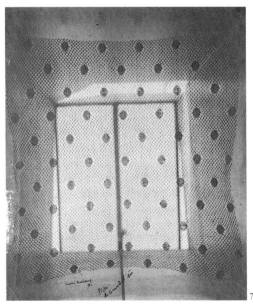

72

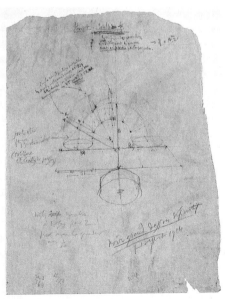

73

74-75. *Trois stoppages-étalon (Three Standard Stoppages)*,
1913-14.
Assemblage: three threads just under 1 metre long fixed to
three strips of canvas (120×13.3 cm each), which are in turn
glued to three glass panels (125.4×18.3 cm each); each panel is
accompanied by a wooden ruler that follows the curve of the
thread. The whole is contained in a wooden box,
129.2×28.2×22.7 cm.
The Museum of Modern Art, New York,
Katherine S. Dreier Bequest, 1953.

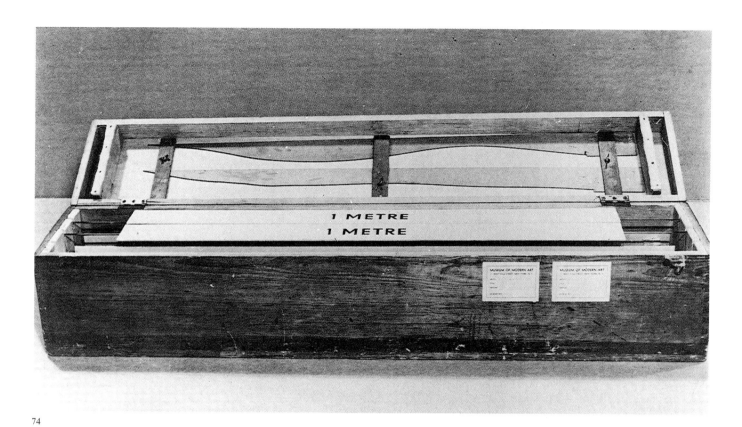

74

75

76. *Bottlerack* or *Bottle Dryer* or *Hedgehog*, replica of lost
original. 1914
Readymade: galvanized iron bottle dryer.
Philadelphia Museum of Art.

77. *In Advance of the Broken Arm*, replica of lost 1915 original.
Readymade: snow-shovel, wood and galvanized iron, height
121.3 cm.
Philadelphia Museum of Art.
The Louise and Walter Arensberg Collection.

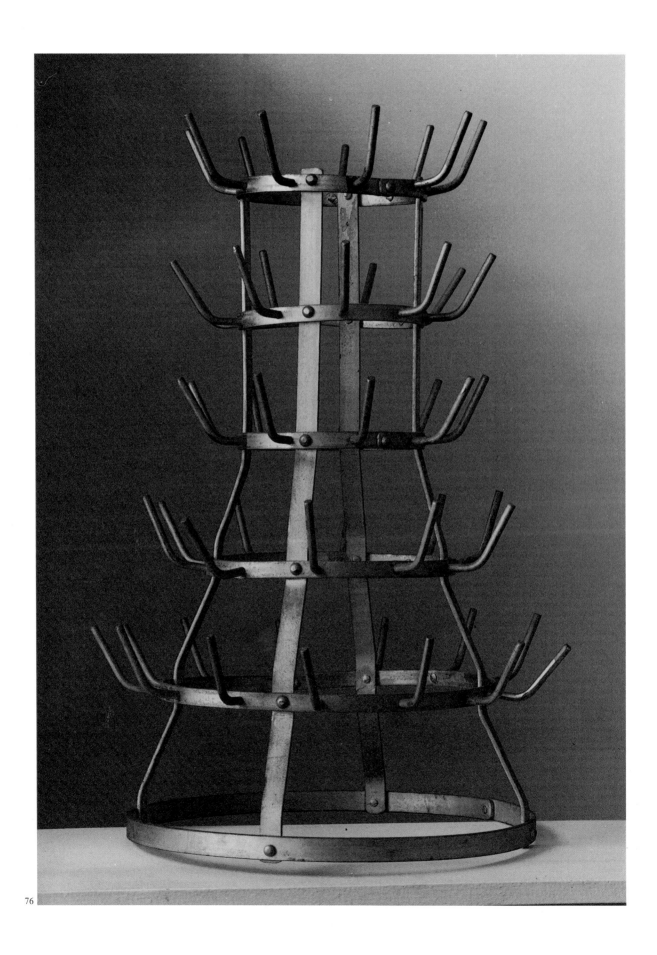

78-79. *The Bride Stripped Bare by her Bachelors, Even (The Large Glass)*, 1915-23.
Oil paint, varnish, lead foil, lead wire and dust on two glass plates (cracked), each mounted between two glass panels in a steel and wood frame, 272.5 × 175.8 cm.
Philadelphia Museum of Art,
The Louise and Walter Arensberg Collection.

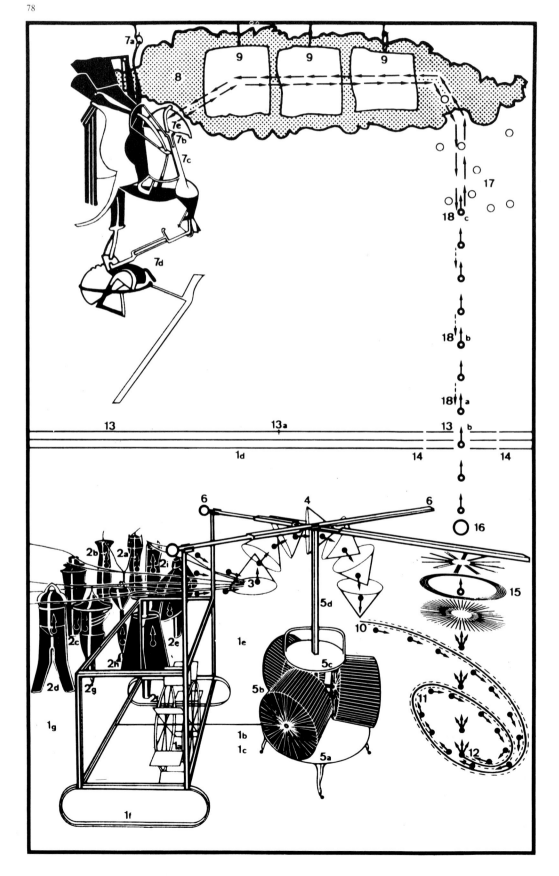

Key to the *Large Glass* (including elements not executed):

1 Chariot or Sleigh
  (a) Water-mill wheel
  (b) Pinion
  (c) Trap-door to basement
  (d) Pulley
  (e) Revolution of the bottle of Bénédictine
  (f) Runners
  (g) Sandow
2 Nine Malic Moulds/Cemetery of Uniforms and Liveries
  (a) Priest
  (b) Delivery boy
  (c) Gendarme
  (d) Cavalryman
  (e) Policeman
  (f) Undertaker
  (g) Servant/Flunky
  (h) Busboy/Waiter's assistant
  (i) Station-master
3 Capillary Tubes
4 Sieves or Parasols
5 Chocolate Grinder
  (a) Louis XV chassis
  (b) Rollers
  (c) Necktie
  (d) Bayonet
6 Scissors
7 The Bride/*Pendu femelle*
  (a) Suspension ring
  (b) Mortice joint
  (c) Stem
  (d) Wasp
8 Milky Way
9 Draught Pistons
10 Region of Butterfly Pump
11 Toboggan or Planes/Slopes of flow
12 Crashes or Splashes
13 Horizon/Bride's garment
  (a) Vanishing point of perspective
  (b) Region of 'Wilson-Lincoln' effect
14 Boxing Match
15 Oculist Witnesses
16 Magnifying glass
17 Nine Shots
18 Handler of Gravity
  (a) Trivet
  (b) Rod
  (c) Weight

●→   path of Illuminating Gas

→   Bride's instructions

After Jean Suquet, *Miroir de la Mariée* (Flammarion).

80. *Comb*, 1916.
   Readymade: grey steel comb, 16.6 × 3.2 cm.
   Philadelphia Museum of Art,
   The Louise and Walter Arensberg Collection.

81. *Rendez-vous of Sunday, February 6, 1916 . . .*, 1916.
   Text typed on four postcards, 28.4 × 14.4 cm overall.
   Philadelphia Museum of Art,
   The Louise and Walter Arensberg Collection.

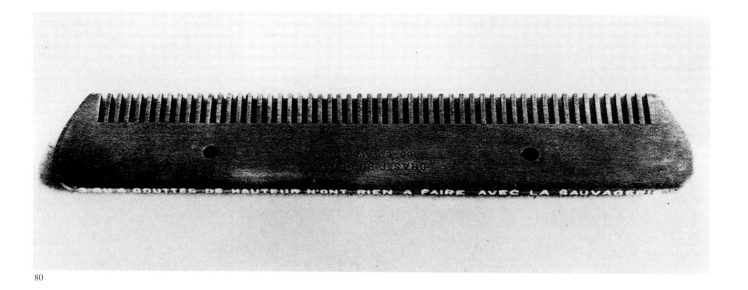

80

81

82

82. *The*, 1915.
Handwritten text, ink on paper, 22.2 × 14.3 cm.
Philadelphia Museum of Art.
The Louise and Walter Arensberg Collection.

83. *With Hidden Noise*, 1916.
Assisted Readymade: ball of string between two unpolished
brass plates joined by four bolts. The ball encloses a small
unknown object (added by Walter Arensberg) which makes a
noise when shaken, 12.9 × 13 × 11.4 cm.
Philadelphia Museum of Art,
The Louise and Walter Arensberg Collection.

83

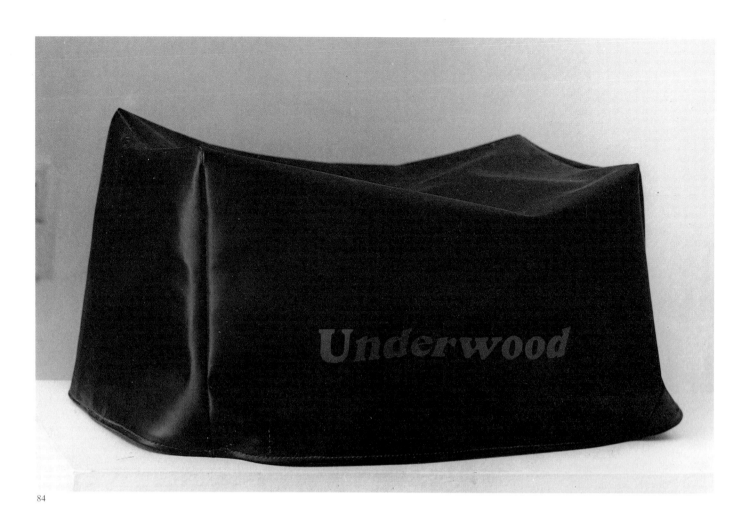

84

85

84. *Traveller's Folding Item*, 1916.
Readymade: Underwood typewriter cover, height 23 cm.
Philadelphia Museum of Art,
The Louise and Walter Arensberg Collection.

85. *Apolinère Enameled*, 1916-17.
Rectified Readymade: pencil on cardboard and painted zinc
plate (advertisement for Sapolin enamel paints), 24.5 × 33.9 cm.
Philadelphia Museum of Art.
The Louise and Walter Arensberg Collection.

86. *Fountain*, 1917 (original lost).
Readymade: porcelain urinal, height 60 cm.
Philadelphia Museum of Art.
The Louise and Walter Arensberg Collection.

86

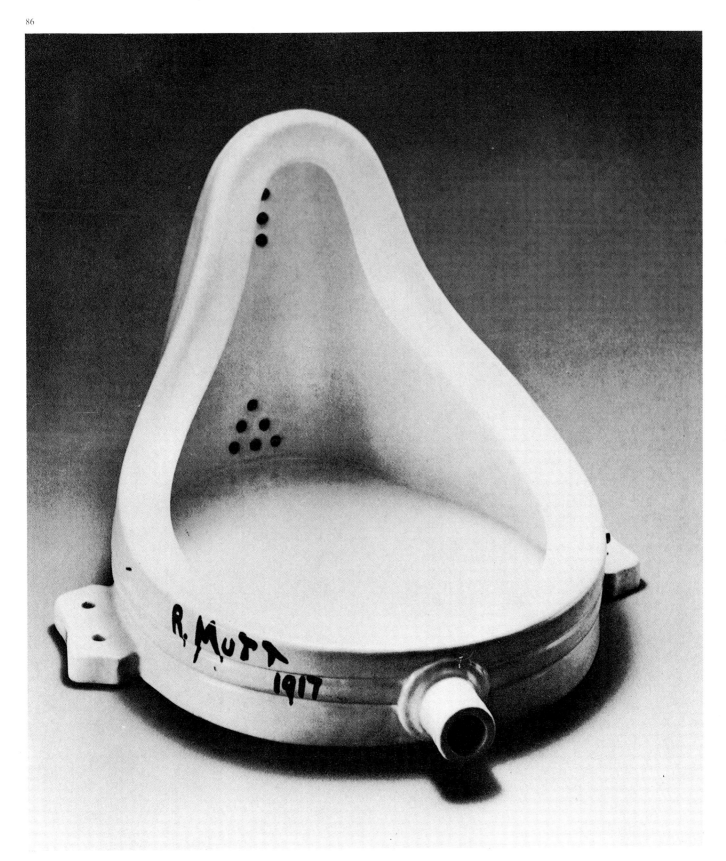

87. *Tu m'*, 1918.
    Oil and pencil on canvas, with bottle-brush, three safety pins
    and a bolt, 69.8 × 313 cm.
    Yale University Art Gallery, New Haven, Conn.
    Bequest of Katherine S. Dreier, 1953.

87

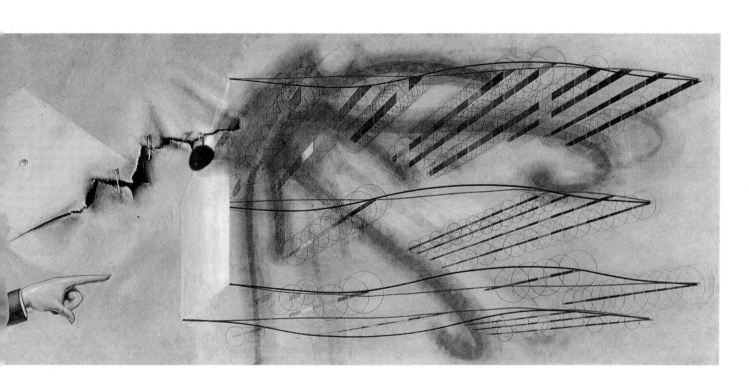

88. *Hat Rack*, 1917 (original lost).
   Readymade: wooden hat rack suspended from the ceiling,
   23.5 × 14 cm.
   Musée National d'Art Moderne, Paris.

89. *Trébuchet (Trap)*, 1917 (original lost).
   Readymade: wood and metal coat rack nailed to the floor,
   11.7 × 100 cm.
   Musée National d'Art Moderne, Paris.

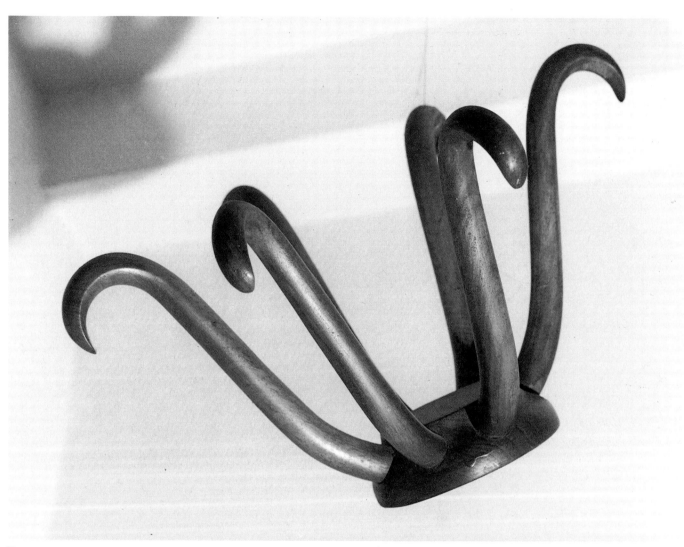

88

90. *Handmade Stereopticon Slides*, 1918-19.
Rectified Readymade: pencil on stereoscopic slides, each
5.7×5.7 cm, in cardboard mount 6.8×17.2 cm overall.
The Museum of Modern Art, New York,
Katherine S. Dreier Bequest, 1953.

91. *Oculist Witnesses*, 1920.
Pointed instrument on the reverse of a sheet of carbon paper,
50×37.5 cm.
Philadelphia Museum of Art,
The Louise and Walter Arensberg Collection.

90

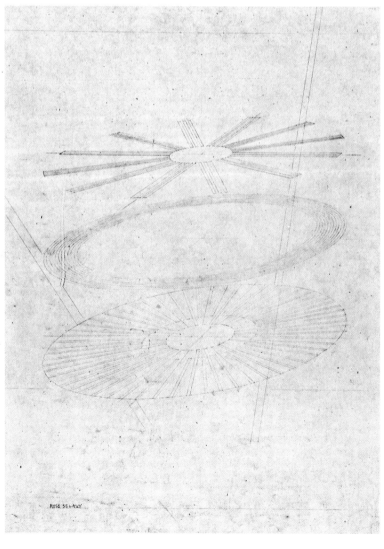

91

92. *To be Looked at (from the Other Side of the Glass) with One
    Eye, Close to, for Almost an Hour*, 1918.
    Oil paint, silver leaf, lead wire, and magnifying glasses on glass
    support (cracked) 49.5 × 39.7 cm, mounted between two glass
    panes in a metal frame, 51 × 41.2 × 3.7 cm, on a painted wood
    base; height overall, 55.8 cm.
    The Museum of Modern Art, New York,
    Katherine S. Dreier Bequest, 1953.

93

93. *50 cc of Paris Air*, 1919.
Readymade: 50 cc glass ampoule, height 13.3 cm.
Philadelphia Museum of Art,
The Louise and Walter Arensberg Collection.

94. *Tzanck Cheque*, 1919.
Ink on paper, 21×38.2 cm.
Galleria Schwarz, Milan.

95. *L.H.O.O.Q.* 1919.
Rectified Readymade: pencil on a reproduction of the
Mona Lisa, 19.7× 12.4 cm.
Private collection, Paris.

94

N.º 4866

Paris December 3rd 1919

The Teeth's Loan & Trust Company, Consolidated
2 Wall Street,
New York.

Pay to the Order of Daniel Tzanck
one hundred fifteen and no/100 Dollars

ORION

Marcel Duchamp

$ 115. 00/100

L.H.O.O.Q.

96-97. *Rotary Glass Plates (Precision Optics)*, 1920.
Five painted glass plates rotating simultaneously on a metal
axis and forming unbroken concentric circles (to be viewed at a
distance of 1 metre); supporting frame 120.6 × 184.1 × 14 cm
and 99 × 14 cm (glass plate).
Yale University Art Gallery, New Haven, Conn.

96

98

98. *Dust Breeding*, 1920.
Photograph by Man Ray, 24×30.5 cm.

99. *Belle Haleine, Eau de Voilette (Beautiful Breath, Veil Water)*, 1921.
Photo-collage, 29.6×20 cm.
Collection Carl Frederick Reutersward, Bussigny, Switzerland.

100. *Belle Haleine, Eau de Voilette*, 1921.
Assisted Readymade: perfume bottle with label, in a
conforming case, 16.3×11.2 cm.
Private collection, Paris.

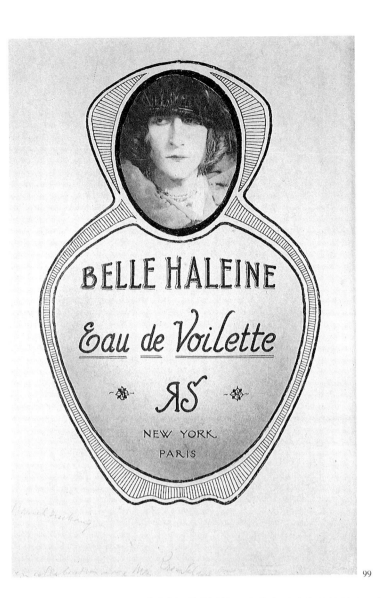

101. *La Bagarre d'Austerlitz (The Brawl at Austerlitz)*, 1921.
Miniature window: oil on wood and glass,
62.8 × 28.7 × 6.3 cm.
Staatsgalerie, Stuttgart.

102. *Fresh Widow*, 1920.
Miniature window: painted wood, and glass panes covered
with squares of polished leather, 77.5 × 45 cm. overall, on a
wooden sill, 1.9 × 53.3 × 10.2 cm.
The Museum of Modern Art, New York,
Katherine S. Dreier Bequest, 1953.

103

103. *Monte Carlo Bond*, 1924.
Photo-collage with photograph of Marcel Duchamp by Man Ray on coloured lithograph, 31 × 19 cm.
The Museum of Modern Art, New York (gift of the artist, 1939).

104. *Discs Bearing Spirals*, 1923.
Ink and pencil on seven roughly cut white paper discs (diameters ranging from 21.6 to 31.7 cm), mounted on blue paper discs, the whole fixed to a sheet of paper, 108.2 × 108.2 cm.
Seattle Art Museum, Seattle.

105. *Rotoreliefs (optical discs)*, 1935.
Six cardboard discs printed on both sides by offset lithography, each 20 cm in diameter.
Private collection, Paris.

106-107. *Anémic Cinéma*, 1925.
(in collaboration with Man Ray and Marc Allégret).
Spiral discs from the black-and-white silent film of 7 minutes' duration.
The Museum of Modern Art, New York.

108. *Japanese Fish* (*Rotoreliefs* series), 1935.
Carboard disc printed on both sides by offset lithography, diameter 20 cm.
The Museum of Modern Art, New York, Gift of Rose Fried.

109. *Lamp* (*Rotoreliefs* series), 1935.
Cardboard disc printed on both sides by offset lithography, diameter 20 cm.
The Museum of Modern Art, New York, Gift of Rose Fried.

104

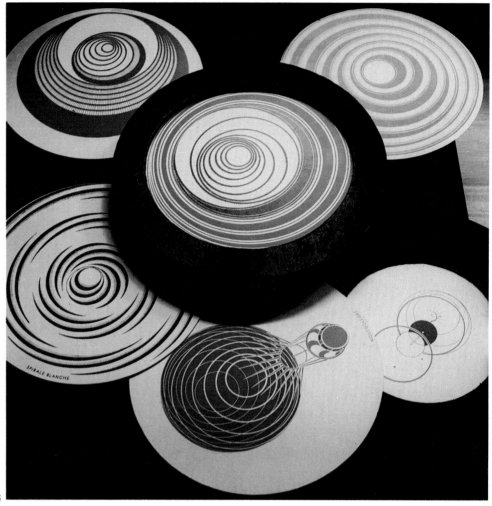

105

106

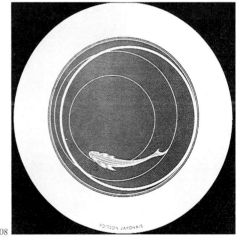

108

107

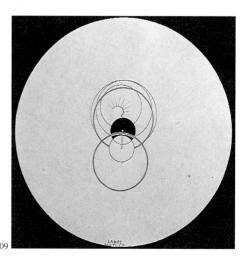

109

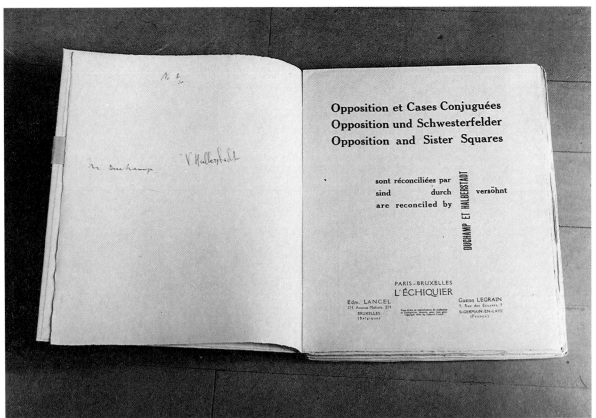

110

111

110. *Opposition and Sister Squares are Reconciled*, 1932.
Treatise on chess in French, German and English,
28 × 24.5 cm.
Private collection, Paris.

111. *The Bride Stripped Bare by her Bachelors, Even
(The Green Box)*, 1934.
93 facsimiles (photographs, drawings and manuscript notes,
1911-15) and a colour plate, all in a green cardboard box.
Standard edition of 300 numbered and signed copies. De luxe
edition of 20 numbered and signed copies, with supplementary
photographs and a page of manuscript. Édition Rrose Sélavy,
Paris, 33.2 × 28 × 2.5 cm.
Private collection, Paris.

112. *Box-in-a-Valise*, 1936-41.
Cardboard box (sometimes inside a leather suitcase)
containing a replica in miniature, photographs and colour
reproductions of works by Duchamp, 40.7 × 38.1 × 10.2 cm.
De luxe edition of 20 copies (the earlier ones include a
celluloid reproduction of the *Glissière contenant un moulin à
eau en métaux voisins* [cf. fig. 62]), numbered I to XX and
signed. Standard edition of 300 copies (unnumbered).
Private collection, Paris.

112

113. *Please Touch*, 1947.
Foam-rubber breast on black velvet mounted on cardboard,
23.5 × 20.5 cm.
Private collection, Paris.

114. *In the Manner of Delvaux*, 1942.
Collage of aluminium foil and photograph on cardboard,
34 × 34 cm.
Collection Arturo Schwarz, Milan.

113

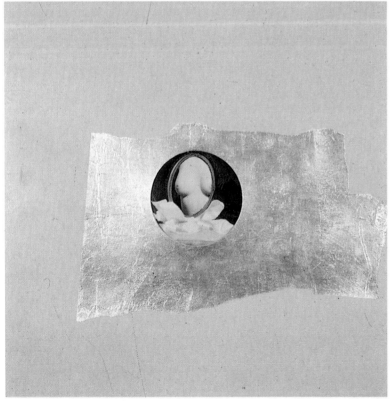

114

115. *Genre Allegory (George Washington)*, 1943.
     Assemblage: cardboard, gauze, nails, iodine, gilt metal stars,
     53.2 × 40.5 cm.
     Musée National d'Art Moderne, Paris.

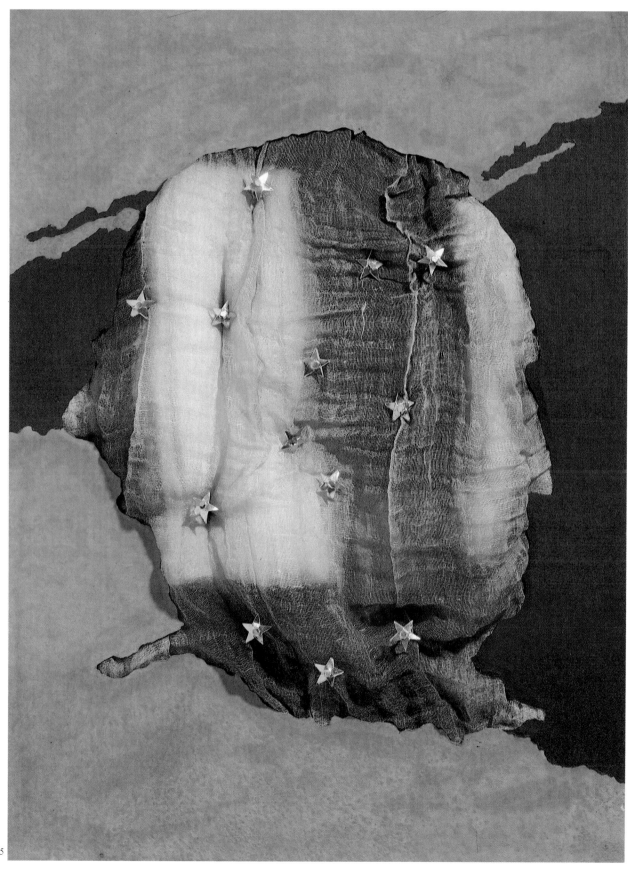

116. *Preparatory Study for the Figure in 'Étant donnés: 1. La chute d'eau, 2. Le gaz d'éclairage', c.* 1950 (cf. fig. 130).
Gouache on transparent perforated plexiglass, 91.3 × 55.9 cm.
Private collection, Paris.

117. *Given the illuminating gas and the waterfall* (preparatory study), 1948-49.
Painted leather on plaster relief, mounted on velvet, 50 × 31 cm.
Moderna Museet, Stockholm.

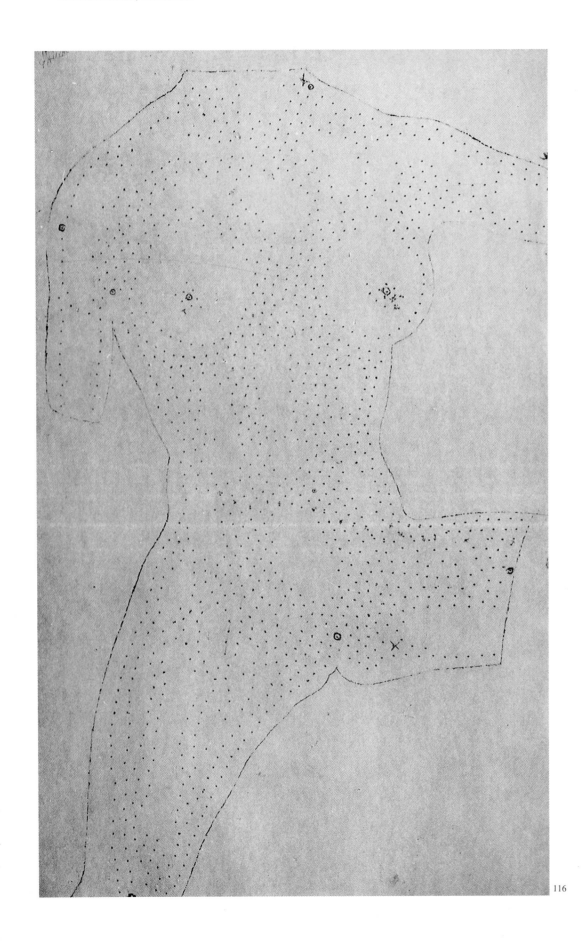

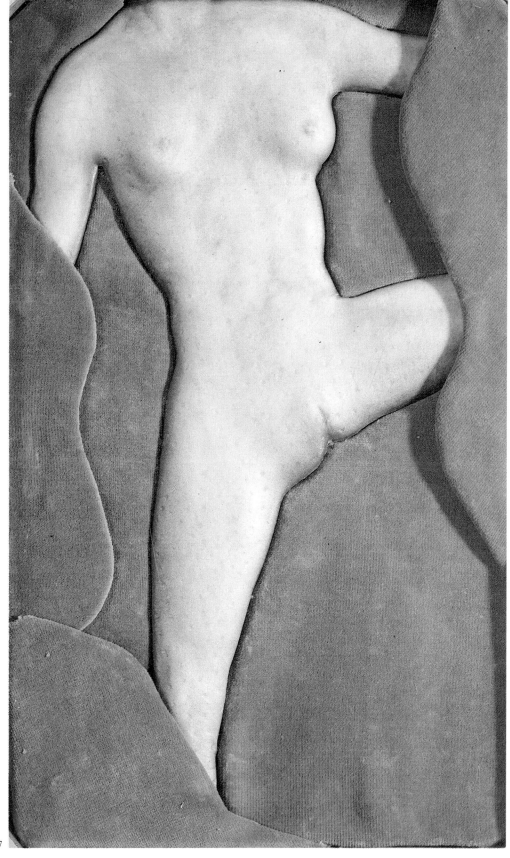

118. *Wedge of Chastity*, 1954.
      Galvanized plaster and plastic, 5.6 × 8.5 × 4.2 cm.
      Private collection, Paris.

119. *Female Fig-leaf*, 1950.
      Galvanized plaster, 9 × 14 × 12.5 cm.
      Private collection, Paris.

120. *Objet-dard (Dart-object)*, 1951.
      Galvanized plaster, 7.5 × 20.1 × 6 cm.
      Private collection, Paris.

118

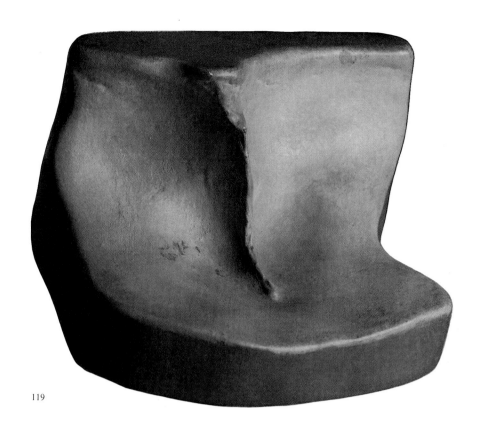

119

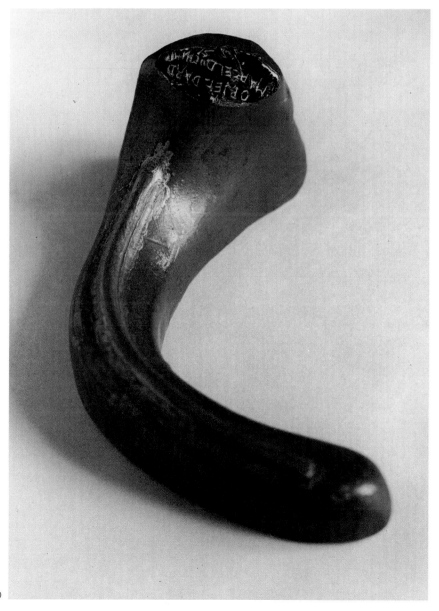

120

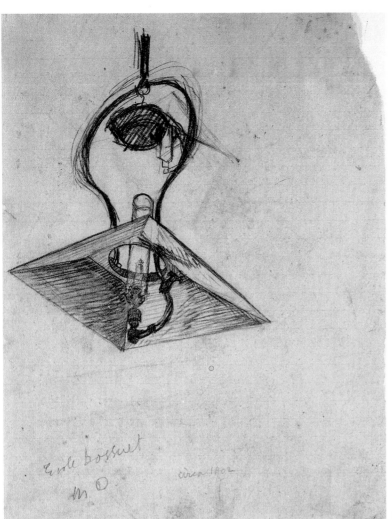

121

121. *Hanging Gas Lamp (Bec Auer)*, 1903-04.
Charcoal drawing, 22.4 × 17.2 cm.
Private collection, Paris.

122. *Water and Gas on Every Floor*, 1958.
Imitated Readymade: white lettering on a blue enamel plaque,
replica of signs in Paris apartment buildings of the turn of
the century, 15 × 20 cm (seen mounted on box for special
edition of Robert Lebel's *Sur Marcel Duchamp*).
Collection Robert Lebel, Paris.

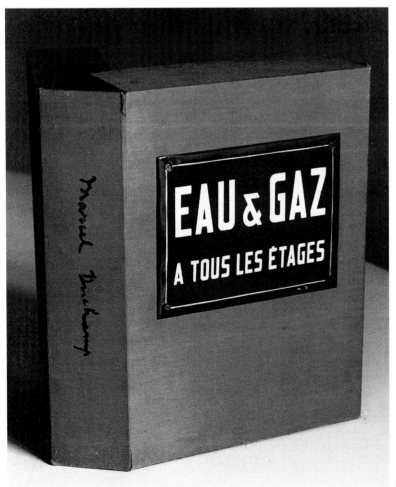

122

123. *Self-portrait in profile*, 1958.
Torn sheet of coloured paper on black background,
14.3 × 12.5 cm.
Collection Robert Lebel, Paris.

124. *Torture-morte (Still-torture)*, 1959.
Painted plaster and flies on paper mounted on wood,
29.5 × 13.5 × 5.5 cm.
Collection Robert Lebel, Paris.

125. *Sculpture-morte (Still-sculpture)*, 1959.
Marzipan and insects on paper, mounted on masonite,
33.5 × 22.5 × 5.5 cm.
Collection Robert Lebel, Paris.

126. *With my Tongue in my Cheek*, 1959.
Plaster, pencil and paper on wood, 25 × 15 × 5.1 cm.
Collection Robert Lebel, Paris.

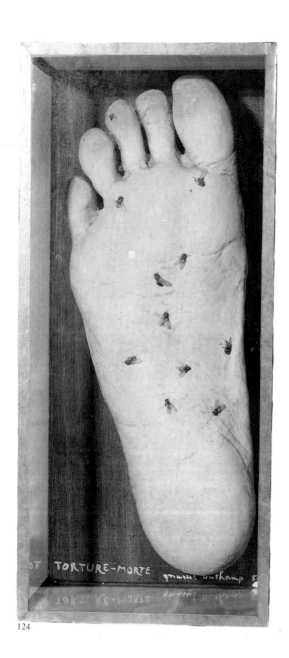

124

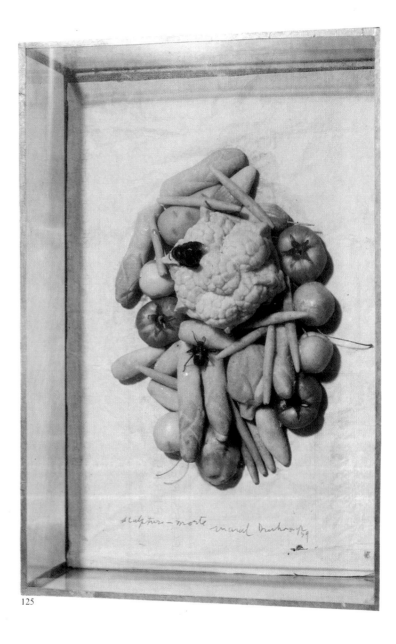

125

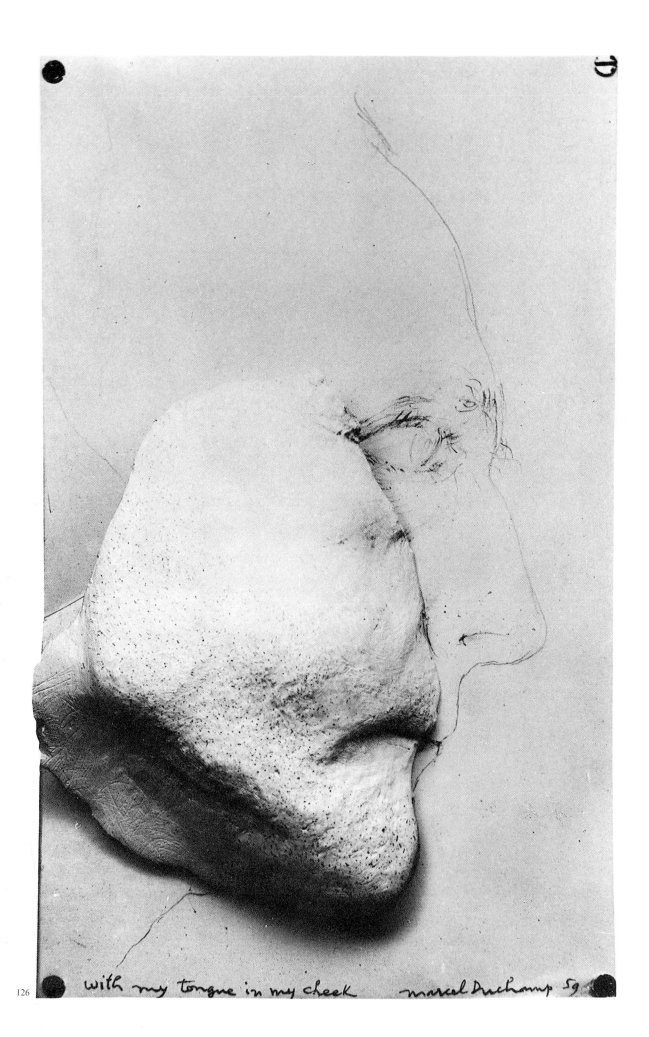

with my tongue in my cheek   marcel duchamp 59

126

127. *Aimer tes héros (Love your Heroes)*, 1963.
Pencil and ink on paper, 31.3 × 26 cm.
Collection Arturo Schwarz, Milan.

128. *Bouche-Évier*, 1964.
Lead bath-plug for Duchamp's apartment in Cadaqués,
diameter 7.5 cm.

129-130. *Étant donnés: 1. La chute d'eau, 2. Le gaz d'éclairage
(Given: 1. The Waterfall, 2. The Illuminating Gas)*, 1946-66.
Mixed media assemblage: an old wooden door, bricks, velvet,
wood, leather stretched over a metal armature, twigs,
aluminium, iron, glass, plexiglass, linoleum, cotton, electric
lamps, gas lamp (Bec Auer type), motor, etc.,
242.5 × 177.8 × 124.5 cm.
Philadelphia Museum of Art, Gift of the Cassandra
Foundation, 1969.

127

128

129

131

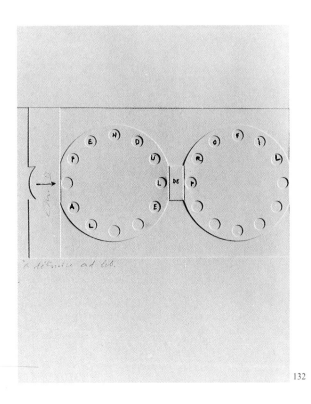

132

131. *À l'Infinitif (La Boîte blanche) / In the Infinitive (The White Box)*, 1967.
79 facsimile notes (dating from 1914-23) in a plexiglass box with a silkscreen reproduction of the *Glissière contenant un moulin à eau* (cf. fig. 62) on the cover, 33.3×29 cm.
Édition of 150 signed and numbered copies.
Private collection, Paris.

132. *Clock in Profile*, 1964.
Thin card, 22×28 cm.
Private collection, Barcelona.

133. *Selected Details after Courbet*, 1968.
Etching (second state) on handmade paper, 42.2×25 cm.
Private collection, Paris.

134. *Selected Details after Cranach*, 1968.
Etching (second state) on handmade paper, 42.2×25 cm.
Private collection, Paris.

135. *The Bec Auer*, 1968.
Etching (second state) on handmade paper, 42.2×25 cm.
Private collection, Paris.

136. *The Bride Stripped Bare*, 1968.
Etching (second state) on handmade paper, 50.5×32.5 cm.
Private collection, Paris.

133

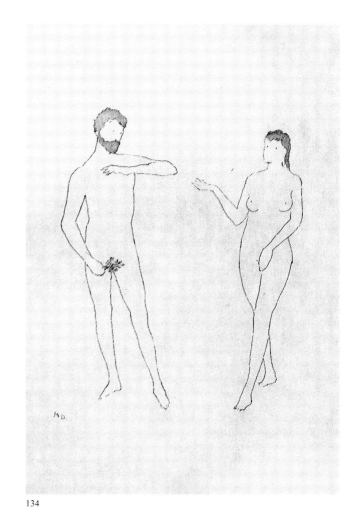

134

135

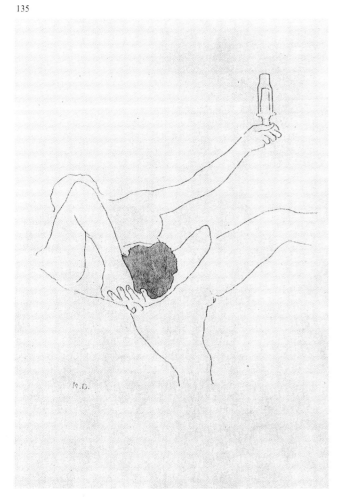

136

LIST OF WORKS ILLUSTRATED

Original French titles are given in parentheses where appropriate; details of medium, size and ownership will be found in individual captions to the illustrations.

1. *Yvonne*, 1902.

2. *Church at Blainville*, 1902.
 (Église à Blainville)

3. *Yvonne (in kimono)*, 1901.
 (Yvonne [en kimono])

4. *Play?*, 1902.

5. *Suzanne Duchamp Seated*, 1903.
 (Suzanne Duchamp assise)

6. *Portrait of Jacques Villon*, 1904-05.
 (Portrait de Jacques Villon)

7. *Parva Domus, Magna Quies*, 1902.

8. *For the Menu of Simone Delacour's First Communion Dinner*, 1909.
 (Pour le menu de dîner de première communion de Simone Delacour)

9. *Portrait of Yvonne Duchamp*, 1909.
 (Portrait d'Yvonne Duchamp)

10. *Man Seated by a Window*, 1907.
 (Homme assis près d'une fenêtre)

11. *Two Nudes*, 1910.
 (Deux nus)

12. *Nude with Black Stockings*, 1910.
 (Nu aux bas noirs)

13. *The Chess Game*, 1910.
 (La Partie d'échecs)

14. *Laundry-barge*, 1910.
 (Bateau-lavoir)

15. *Portrait of the Artist's Father*, 1910.
 (Portrait du père de l'artiste)

16. *Portrait of Dr Dumouchel*, 1910.
 (Portrait du docteur Dumouchel)

17. *Portrait bust of Chauvel*, 1910.
 (Portrait en buste de Chauvel)

18. *Portrait of Dr Ferdinand Tribout*, 1910.
 (Portrait du docteur Ferdinand Tribout)

19. *Standing Nude*, 1910.
 (Nu debout)

20. *The Bush*, 1910-11.
 (Le buisson)

21. *Baptism*, 1911.
 (Baptême)

22. *Nude on Nude*, 1910-11.
 (Nu sur nu)

23. *Draught on the Japanese Apple Tree*, 1911.
 (Courant d'air sur le pommier du Japon)

24. *Paradise*, 1910-11.
 (Paradis)

25. *Landscape*, 1911.
 (Paysage)

26. *Apropos of Little Sister*, 1911.
 (À propos de Jeune Sœur)

27. *Yvonne and Magdeleine in Tatters*, 1911.
 (Yvonne et Magdeleine déchiquetées)

28. *Sonata*, 1911.
 (Sonate)

29. *Dulcinea*, 1911.
 (Portrait ou Dulcinée)

30. *Mediocrity*, 1911.
 (Médiocrité)

31. *Study for 'Portrait of Chess Players'*, 1911.
 (Étude pour le Portrait de joueurs d'échecs)

32. *The Chess Players*, 1911.
 (Les Joueurs d'échecs)

33. *Study for 'Portrait of Chess Players'*, 1911.
 (Étude pour les Joueurs d'échecs)

34. *Study for 'Portrait of Chess Players'* or *For a Game of Chess*, 1911.
 (Étude pour les Joueurs d'échecs ou Pour une partie d'échecs)

35. *Portrait of Chess Players*, 1911.
 (Portrait de joueurs d'échecs)

36. *Coffee Mill*, 1911.
 (Moulin à café)

37. *Coffee Mill*, 1911.
 (Moulin à café)

38. *Young Man and Girl in Spring*, 1911.
 (Jeune Homme et jeune fille dans le printemps)

39. *Sad Young Man in a Train*, 1911.
 (Jeune Homme triste dans un train)

40. *Nude on a Ladder*, 1907-08.
 (Nu sur une échelle)

41. *Nude on a Ladder*, 1907-08.

42. *Nude Descending a Staircase, No. 2*, 1912.
 (Nu descendant un escalier, n° 2)

43. *Portrait of Gustave Candel's Mother*, 1911-12.
 (Portrait de la mère de Gustave Candel)

44. *Two Nudes: One Strong and One Swift*, 1912.
 (Deux Nus: un fort et un vite)

45. *Two Personages and a Car (Study)*, 1912.
 (Deux personnages et une auto [étude])

46. *The King and Queen Traversed by Swift Nudes*, 1912.
 (Le Roi et la Reine traversés par des nus vites)

47. *The Bride Stripped Bare by the Bachelors*, 1912.
 (La Mariée mise à nu par les célibataires)

48. *The King and Queen Traversed by Nudes at High Speed*, 1912.
 (Le Roi et la Reine traversés par des nus en vitesse)

49. *The King and Queen Surrounded by Swift Nudes*, 1912.
 (Le Roi et la Reine entourés de nus vites)

50. *The Passage from Virgin to Bride*, 1912.
 (Le passage de la vierge à la mariée)

51. *Virgin, No. 1*, 1912.
   (Vierge, n° 1)

52. *Virgin, No. 2*, 1912.
   (Vierge, n° 2)

53. *Bride*, 1912.
   (Mariée)

54. *Bachelor Apparatus (plan)*, 1913.
   (Machine célibataire [plan])

55. *Bachelor Apparatus (elevation)*, 1913.
   (Machine célibataire [élévation])

56. *Boxing Match*, 1913.
   (Combat de boxe)

57. *The Bride Stripped Bare by her Bachelors, Even*, 1913.
   (La Mariée mise à nu par ses célibataires, même)

58. *Cemetery of Uniforms and Liveries, No. 1*, 1913.
   (Cimetière des uniformes et livrées, n° 1)

59. *The Knife-grinder*, 1904-05.
   (Le Remouleur)

60. *Studies for the Bachelors: Station-master*, 1913.
   (Chef de gare. Premières etudes pour les célibataires)

61. *Nine Malic Moulds*, 1914-15.
   (9 Moules malic)

62. *Glider Containing a Water Mill in Neighbouring Metals*, 1913-15.
   (Glissière contenant un moulin à eau en métaux voisins)

63. *Musical Erratum*, 1913.
   (Erratum musical)

64. *Perspective Drawing for the Water-mill Wheel*, 1913.
   (Dessin perspectif pour la roue du moulin)

65. *Bicycle Wheel*, 1913.
   (Roue de bicyclette)

66. *The Box of 1914*, 1913-14.
   (La Boîte de 1914)

67. *Pharmacy*, 1914.
   (Pharmacie)

68. *To Have the Apprentice in the Sun*, 1914.
   (Avoir l'Apprenti dans le soleil)

69. *Study for the 'Chocolate Grinder, No. 2'*, 1914.
   (Étude pour la Broyeuse de chocolat, n° 2)

70. *Chocolate Grinder, No. 2*, 1914.
   (Broyeuse de chocolat, n° 2)

71. *Réseaux des stoppages (Network of Stoppages)*, 1914.

72. *Draught Piston*, 1914.
   (Piston de courant d'air)

73. *First Study for the Sieves*, 1914.
   (Première étude pour les tamis)

74-75. *Trois stoppages-étalon (Three Standard Stoppages)*, 1913-14.

76. *Bottlerack* or *Bottle Dryer* or *Hedgehog*, 1914.
   (Porte-bouteilles ou Séchoir à bouteilles ou Hérisson)

77. *In Advance of the Broken Arm*, 1915.

78-79. *The Bride Stripped Bare by her Bachelors, Even (The Large Glass)*, 1915-23.
   (La Mariée mise à nu par ses célibataires, même)

80. *Comb*, 1916.
   (Peigne)

81. *Rendez-vous of Sunday, February 6, 1916 . . .*, 1916.
   (Rendez-vous du dimanche 6 février 1916 . . .)

82. *The*, 1915.

83. *With Hidden Noise*, 1916.
   (À bruit secret)

84. *Traveller's Folding Item*, 1916.
   (Pliant . . . de voyage)

85. *Apolinère Enameled*, 1916-17.

86. *Fountain*, 1917.

87. *Tu m'*, 1918.

88. *Hat Rack*, 1917.
   (Porte-chapeau)

89. *Trébuchet (Trap)*, 1917.

90. *Handmade Stereopticon Slides*, 1918-19.
   (Stéréoscopie à la main)

91. *Oculist Witnesses*, 1920.
   (Témoins oculistes)

92. *To be Looked at (from the Other Side of the Glass) with One Eye, Close to, for Almost an Hour*, 1918.
   (À regarder [l'autre côté du verre] d'un œil, de près, pendant presque une heure)

93. *50 cc of Paris Air*, 1919.
   (Air de Paris)

94. *Tzanck Cheque*, 1919.

95. *L.H.O.O.Q.*, 1919.

96-97. *Rotary Glass Plates (Precision Optics)*, 1920.
   (Rotative plaque verre [optique de précision])

98. *Dust Breeding*, 1920.
   (Élevage de poussière)

99. *Belle Haleine, Eau de Voilette (Beautiful Breath, Veil Water)*, photo-collage, 1921.

100. *Belle Haleine, Eau de Voilette*, 1921.

101. *La Bagarre d'Austerlitz (The Brawl at Austerlitz)*, 1921.

102. *Fresh Widow*, 1920.

103. *Monte Carlo Bond*, 1924.
   (Obligations pour la roulette de Monte-Carlo)

104. *Discs Bearing Spirals*, 1923.
   (Disques avec spirales)

105. *Rotoreliefs (optical discs)*, 1935.
   (Rotoreliefs [Disques optiques])

106-107. *Anémic Cinéma*, 1925.

108. *Japanese Fish (Rotoreliefs series)*, 1935.
    (Poisson japonais)

109. *Lamp (Rotoreliefs series)*, 1935.
    (Lampe)

110. *Opposition and Sister Squares are Reconciled*, 1932.
    (L'Opposition et les cases conjuguées sont réconciliées)

111. *The Bride Stripped Bare by her Bachelors, Even (The Green Box)*, 1934.
    (La Mariée mise à nu par ses célibataires, même [La Boîte Verte])

112. *Box-in-a-Valise*, 1936-41.
    (La Boîte-en-valise)

113. *Please Touch*, 1947.
    (Prière de toucher)

114. *In the Manner of Delvaux*, 1942.
    (À la manière de Delvaux)

115. *Genre Allegory (George Washington)*, 1943.
    (Allégorie de genre [George Washington])

116. *Preparatory Study for the Figure in 'Étant donnés: 1. La chute d'eau, 2. Le gaz d'éclairage'*, c. 1950.
    (Étude préparatoire pour la figure dans 'Étant donnés: 1° La chute d'eau; 2° Le gaz d'éclairage)

117. *Given the illuminating gas and the waterfall* (preparatory study), 1948-49.
    (Étant donnés le gaz d'éclairage et la chute d'eau)

118. *Wedge of Chastity*, 1954.
    (Coin de chasteté)

119. *Female Fig-leaf*, 1950.
    (Feuille de vigne femelle)

120. *Objet-dard (Dart-object)*, 1951.

121. *Hanging Gas Lamp (Bec Auer)*, 1903-04.
    (La Suspension [Bec Auer])

122. *Water and Gas on Every Floor*, 1958.
    (Eau et gaz à tous les étages)

123. *Self-portrait in profile*, 1958.
    (Autoportrait de profil)

124. *Torture-morte (Still-torture)*, 1959.

125. *Sculpture-morte (Still-sculpture)*, 1959.

126. *With my Tongue in my Cheek*, 1959.

127. *Aimer tes héros (Love your Heroes)*, 1963.

128. *Bouche-Évier*, 1964.

129-130. *Étant donnés: 1. La chute d'eau, 2. Le gaz d'éclairage (Given: 1. The Waterfall, 2. The Illuminating Gas)*, 1946-66.

131. *À l'Infinitif (La Boîte blanche) / In the Infinitive (The White Box)*, 1967.

132. *Clock in Profile*, 1964.
    (Pendule de profil)

133. *Selected Details after Courbet*, 1968.
    (Morceaux choisis d'après Courbet)

134. *Selected Details after Cranach*, 1968.
    (Morceaux choisis d'après Cranach)

135. *The Bec Auer*, 1968.

136. *The Bride Stripped Bare*, 1968.
    (La Mariée mise à nu)